STAR WARS™

KIRIGAMI

Marc HAGAN-GUIREY

Photos by John GODWIN

CHRONICLE BOOKS
SAN FRANCISCO

INTRODUCTION

If I told my younger self that sometime in the future, I'd find myself standing on the set of a new *Star Wars* film casually talking to J.J. Abrams about my work, he'd be in utter disbelief. He'd probably then ask who the heck J.J. Abrams was. Nonetheless, this came true. All of it.

In November 2014, I was privileged enough to be invited to Pinewood Studios for a tour of *The Force Awakens* sets while they were filming some final pickups. I'd been through Maz's Castle, sat in the actual *Millennium Falcon* cockpit (of course I demonstrated the sequence of buttons, switches and levers required to jump into hyperspace) and played with the real BB-8. In the creature department I'd spotted animatronic masks for Admiral Ackbar, Nien Nunb, and the charred remains of Darth Vader's helmet, long before it had appeared on any teaser or trailer. I was dumbfounded and kept reminding myself to absorb every detail. This was a once in a lifetime experience.

Toward the end of the tour, I found myself standing in a corridor of Starkiller Base. At the far end J.J. Abrams was directing pick-ups with Harrison Ford, Daisy Ridley, and John Boyega. This day couldn't get any better, I thought. As I awkwardly shuffled myself around, trying not to get in the way and apologizing if I found myself within even a five-foot radius of anyone working, my center of goof-filled gravity, or "Murphy's Law" if you will, I somehow found myself face-to-face with J.J. "I'm so sorry." I declared. But as much to my delight as shock, instead of brushing past me toward the more interesting people in the group, we began chatting. He asked me what line of work I was in to which I replied "I'm a designer but my passion is now papercraft, specifically kirigami." His eyes lit up. "I love paper craft! What sort of things do you make?" he asked. "Erm . . . *Star Wars*," I replied.

I started making kirigami in 2012, having been inspired by a visit to Frank Lloyd Wright's Ennis House in Los Angeles; a monumental piece of architecture that was used as a primary location in Ridley Scott's 1982 science-fiction classic, *Blade Runner*. The building, which at the time was very decayed and fragile, inspired me to create a replica in synthetic material—the fragility of paper felt appropriate. After a successful first attempt I began expanding my repertoire, producing my first collection *Horrorgami: 13 Haunted Locations from Film and TV.*

The response to the work was overwhelmingly positive and it began to spread virally across the net. I'd had a zeitgeist moment and very quickly doors to solo exhibitions, commercial commissions and publishing deals began to open. And while I was incredibly busy with this work I was also desperate to start creating *Star Wars*–inspired kirigami. After two years, I finally had the time to dedicate myself to it and in the summer of 2015, opened an exhibition of *Star Wars* Kirigami entitled *Cut Scene*.

I was too young by a few years to have caught the original *Star Wars* wave. My brother however, five years my senior, was the right age. Being born in 1981, my exposure to it was via his dodgy VHS recordings from the television (we'd try and pause the recording during commercial breaks so you'd get a seamless viewing experience) and my (his) collection of Kenner action figures. Like any younger sibling, I commandeered these as my own. It wasn't until I was in my teens that I really understood the flow of the films. I would skip through the majority of *The Empire Strikes Back* in search of the Emperor's death scene, having confused the words "Empire" and "Emperor." Nor did I really comprehend that the Death Star II was not the Death Star I before it was finished. I'm actually envious of anyone who gets to watch the saga for the first time rather than the muddled exposure I'd had. Either way, *Star Wars* was just there from the start of my life like a family member, so to find myself standing on a *Star Wars* set, nevermind talking to the director, was something I'd never expect to have happened.

Within minutes of chatting with J.J., we were swiping through pictures of my kirigami work on my phone. Suddenly he paused and said, "You have got to meet Kathy, she will love this" and just like that I was spun on my heels and frogmarched through Starkiller Base toward Kathleen Kennedy.

"Kathy, this is Marc. He makes amazing stuff. Lucasfilm have got to work with him" interrupts J.J. The next bit is a blur. We chatted for a few minutes. It started with her remarking that she was aware of my work from a conversation I'd had with her office a while ago and ended with her asking how I could be contacted. Miraculously, it was possibly the only time I've ever had a business card in my wallet. As I handed over the tattered, cheap card, I recoiled with embarrassment thinking "This is dismal for a man who calls himself a paper artist."

Marc HAGAN-GUIREY

BEFORE YOU START

Make sure you have all of the recommended tools at hand. Work in a well-lit room and set aside a couple of hours for each project. You might want to put on some music when you're working; I love listening to film soundtracks. John Williams comes highly recommended. Most importantly, take your time and have lots of breaks in between. Cutting on such a small scale can be tiring for the eyes so take a few breaks when you feel you're losing a bit of focus and come back to your project when ready.

Mistakes will happen but don't worry! Carry on as usual and use a bit of sticky tape to put it back together. It might be a good idea to preserve the book by using a photocopier to duplicate the templates. That way, if you make a big mistake, you can start again.

PAPER

The weight of the paper (or gsm) is incredibly important when making kirigami. The templates in this book are printed on 200 gsm (135 lb.) measurements.

If you plan to photocopy the templates, use a paper weight somewhere close to those measurements.

TOOLS

X-ACTO knife and blades - These are easy to get hold of from any art and craft shop. Always use a sharp one as it makes cutting much easier.

Self-healing cutting mat - I once scored the dining table because I didn't use a cutting mat. My mom was not pleased. Not only will a cutting mat protect the work surface but it will also prolong the life of your blades.

Metal ruler - When I've used plastic rulers I've found the knife can accidental slip so invest in a decent metal one. Keep the underside of the ruler clean as a buildup of grime may smudge your nice clean paper.

Skewers - Food skewers or toothpicks are really useful for popping out small creases. They'll also stop folds from wrongly inverting in on themselves as you fold opposing planes.

TEMPLATE FEATURES

Each model comes with some cutting and folding guides. I'll use some terminology when describing them so make sure you familiarize yourself with the following terms.

Template - The template is printed on the reverse of the model. When you display it, you'll be looking at the non-printed side of the paper.

Horizon - This is the central fold of the model. It forms the flat base that the model sits on and the vertical upright part of the model. In simpler terms it's the fold between the sky and the land of the finished model.

Base plate - This is the floor or ground on which the model stands.

Background plate - This is section of the paper standing perpendicular to the base.

CUTTING TERMINOLOGY AND TECHNIQUES

Cutting - Cut all the way through the lines that are printed in black. It's best to start cutting the inner details of the model such as windows, panelling details, and stars. There are a few ways in which you can cut out stars. You can buy a set of tools called "mini hole punches" that create delightfully perfect circles. You could perhaps use a pin and puncture the paper giving it the desired effect, or simply freestyle it. I must add that the stars printed on the template are only a guide and you can cut as few or as many as you like.

Half-cutting - Scoring a line that only cuts halfway through the paper. This makes it easy for the paper to fold making a hinge at 90º. Experiment half-cutting on some paper of a similar weight to the models so you can master the amount of pressure needed.

Valley folds (blue dashed lines) are half-cut on the printed side of the template. The fold is pushed inward like a valley.

Mountain folds (red dotted lines) are half-cut on the non-printed side and pushed outward like a mountain. Because the template is only printed on one side, make some small incisions with the tip of the blade on the back of the card, marking where you need to perform the half-cut. Flip the paper and line up your ruler between these two points and perform the half-cut.

FOLDING TERMINOLOGY AND TECHNIQUES

Never crease the folds fully in the first instance. Gently work your way around the various folds of the model, returning to the beginning and applying a little more pressure to the crease each time. Most of the time, the best method for folding a crease will feel very intuitive.

Levering - Using a forefinger behind the fold as a lever, push down the background plane with your forefinger and base plane with your thumb in the other hand.

Push out - Holding the model in one hand, use the fingers of the other to push one side of the paper along the fold.

Skewer - This technique is essentially the same as levering but where the space is too small to fit your finger in; you can use a skewer to pop elements out.

Pinch - Although I'll rarely recommend pinching the crease, sometimes this is perfectly acceptable to use on smaller mountain or valley folds.

Flatten - Toward the end of each project, once you've been around the folds a few times, fold the model flat and smooth over it with your hand. You can then open it and fix it upright into its display position.

PHOTOGRAPHING YOUR KIRIGAMI MODELS

One of the major aspects I enjoy from making kirigami is the dual personality of paper. Throughout the design process I love how I can manipulate a single sheet of paper into a three-dimensional structure. You learn the properties of the paper and its limitations. Its alter ego however, provides a different kind of thrill; when you are ready to display your model, that's when the fun starts. Once the model is lit, the paper becomes theatrical. It's no longer just a piece of paper—it's a scene with a story. Lighting the model is almost like shooting your own mini movie scene. The mood can be entirely affected by how much light and shadow and even the colors are used; red for danger and war, or blue for a peaceful flight through hyperspace? Lighting is as much an essential part of creating the right tone on a movie set as it is with photographing your model.

The picture below is a suggestion of how you can light yours. Use a colored gel (a lighting term for a sheet of plastic that goes over a light source and acts as a filter) to add depth to the photograph. In addition, use a larger sheet of colored paper to create an infinity backdrop.

PODRACE CRASH, CONCEPT PAINTING BY DOUG CHIANG.

ANAKIN IS PILOTING HIS PODRACER DURING THE BOONTA EVE CLASSIC ON TATOOINE,
STAR WARS: EPISODE I *THE PHANTOM MENACE* (1999).

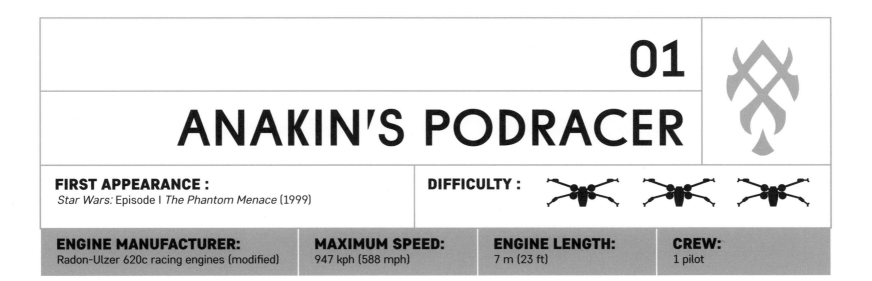

01

ANAKIN'S PODRACER

FIRST APPEARANCE :
Star Wars: Episode I *The Phantom Menace* (1999)

DIFFICULTY :

ENGINE MANUFACTURER:	MAXIMUM SPEED:	ENGINE LENGTH:	CREW:
Radon-Ulzer 620c racing engines (modified)	947 kph (588 mph)	7 m (23 ft)	1 pilot

IN MAY 1999, ALMOST 16 YEARS AFTER THE RELEASE OF *RETURN OF THE JEDI*, GEORGE LUCAS BROUGHT US CRASHING BACK INTO THE *STAR WARS* GALAXY WITH EPISODE I: *THE PHANTOM MENACE.*

As possibly one of the most anticipated films of all time, the stakes were high and Industrial Light & Magic was under insurmountable pressure to deliver a most remarkable visual spectacle. One of the most important sequences undoubtedly takes place at the Mos Espa Grand Arena where we see podracers hurtle across the desert at breakneck speeds of up to 947 kilometers (588 miles) per hour.

The most magical aspect of the podrace sequence is the design of the podracers themselves; the concept team, headed by Doug Chiang, proved themselves to be science-fiction visionaries. Within a huge arena surveyed by Jabba himself, the scene is reminiscent of the classic movie *Ben Hur* set in the Roman era. Podracers are a fantastical blend of the Antiquity and advanced technology: levitating cockpits in place of Roman chariots and, rather than horses pulling Anakin through the desert, two equally erratic turbine engines are tethered to his pod. This mix of the familiar yet foreign design keeps fans intrigued by the *Star Wars* galaxy.

Practical and digital methods were adopted in creating all aspects of the podracers sequence. The racing scenes were created mostly using pioneering computer-generated imagery (CGI) at ILM. Nine of the podracers were life-size constructions used for close-up cockpit shots and background props for the various hanger and race line moments. Credit is also due to the huge miniature model of the arena built for the fly-over shots. If the pressure to produce convincing CGI wasn't already enough, filming wasn't without its problems, too. On day two of shooting in the Tunisian, desert, an uncharacteristically violent storm ravaged the set overnight resulting in most of the life-sized set piece engines being destroyed.

Unfortunately in kirigami we can't rely on green screen and postproduction to create the illusion of a floating ship, so for this design I've worked with the desert environment of jagged rocks to help elevate the vehicle off the ground. For extra support, I made use of the volatile beams cast between the energy binders. Best warn Jar Jar before he starts cutting those out.

Anakin built his podracer himself, and like most pilots he made major customizations using salvaged parts. Although leaner than most other podracers, combined with his skill as a pilot and genius as an engineer, we saw him defeat Sebulba during the Boonta Eve Classic Race, despite Sebulba's brazen violation of the rules.

01
—

ANAKIN'S PODRACER

CUTTING TIPS

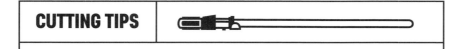

Cut and score the template as per the guide section at the beginning of the book. Start by cutting out the smaller details such as the jagged beams between the energy binders, the twin suns, and the cavities in the rock formations.

FOLDING TIPS

1

With the printed side facing you, start by pushing outward the *valley folds* of the rock formations. If you've *half-cut* the folds correctly, you'll notice the *mountain folds* on the opposite side will start to naturally form.

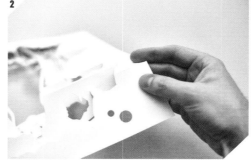

2

Flip the model 180° and push out the *valley folds* on the background plate as well as the central *horizon lines*.

3

Turn the model over to the non-printed side and gradually work around the *mountain folds* using a skewer.

4

To form the engines, hold the base of the engine in one hand and pull the top part toward you with your other hand.

5

Carefully *pinch* together the two small *mountain folds* on the energy beams before folding the whole model flat.

6

Finally tilt upward the two *mountain folds* on either side of the cockpit of the podracer.

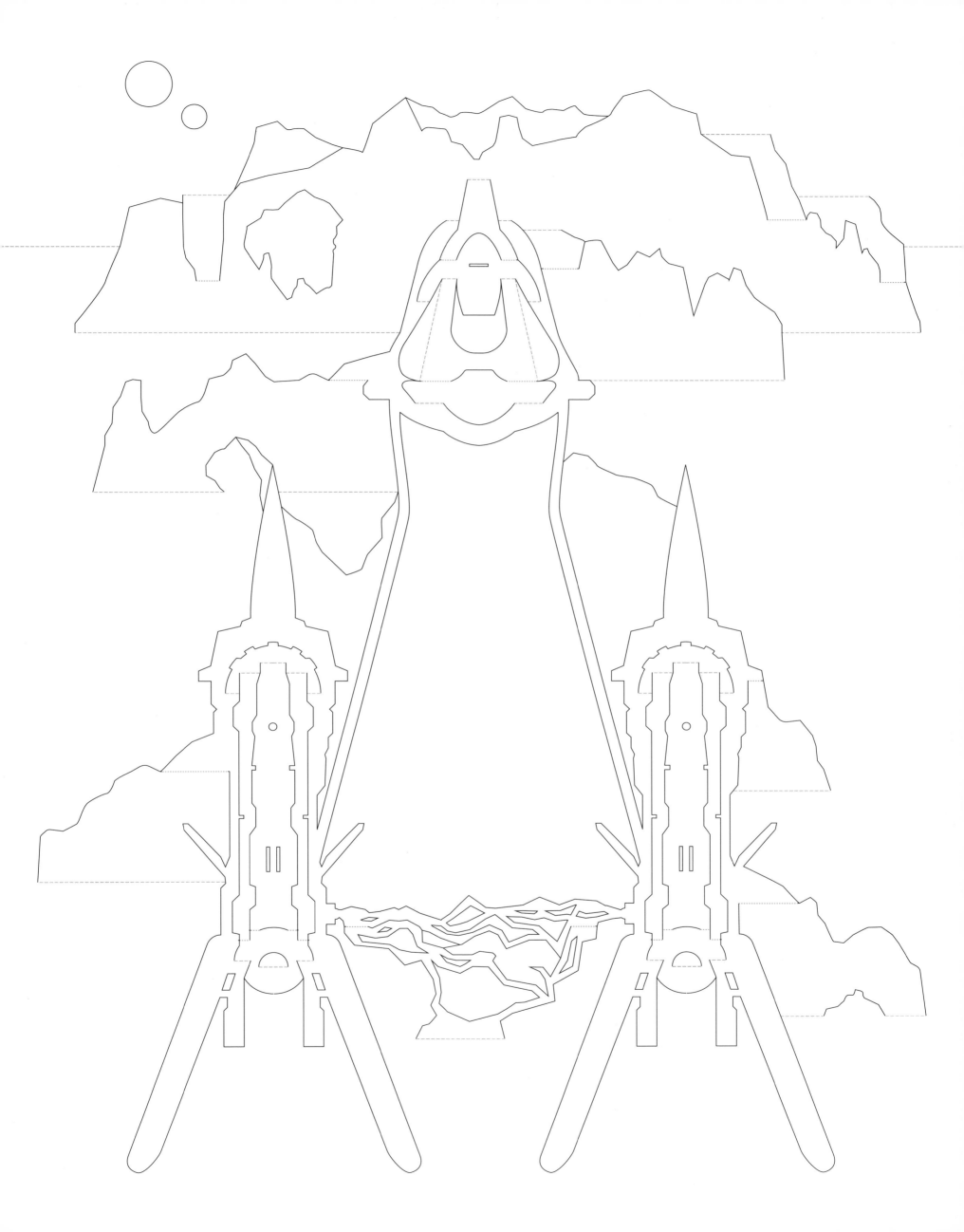

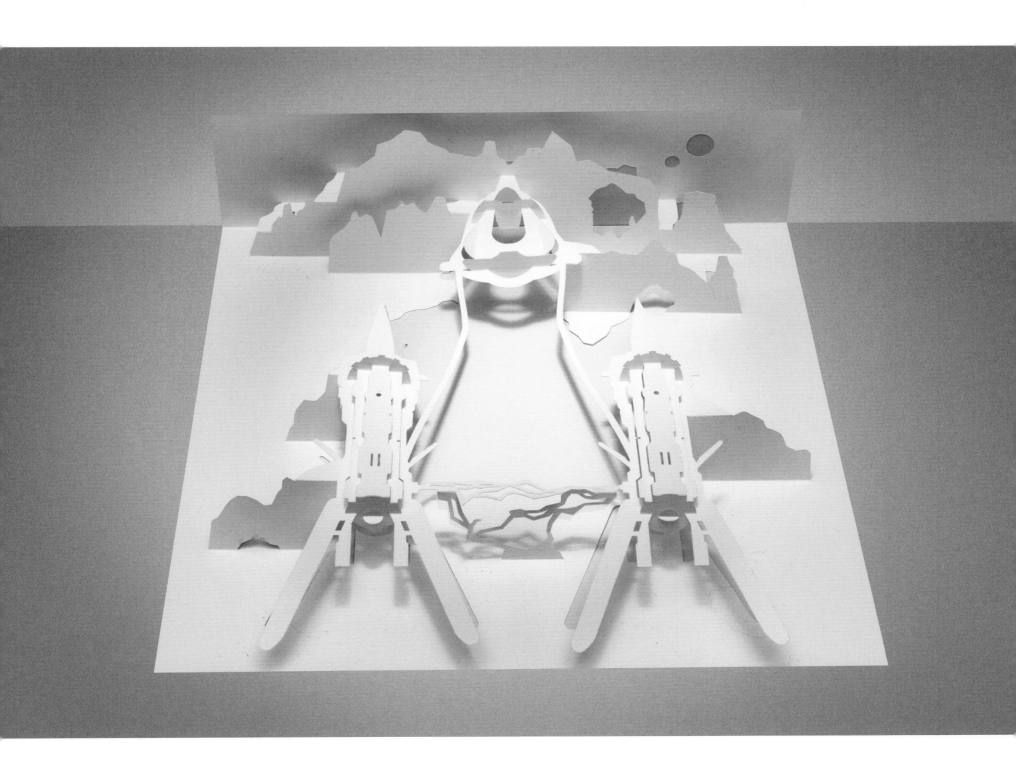

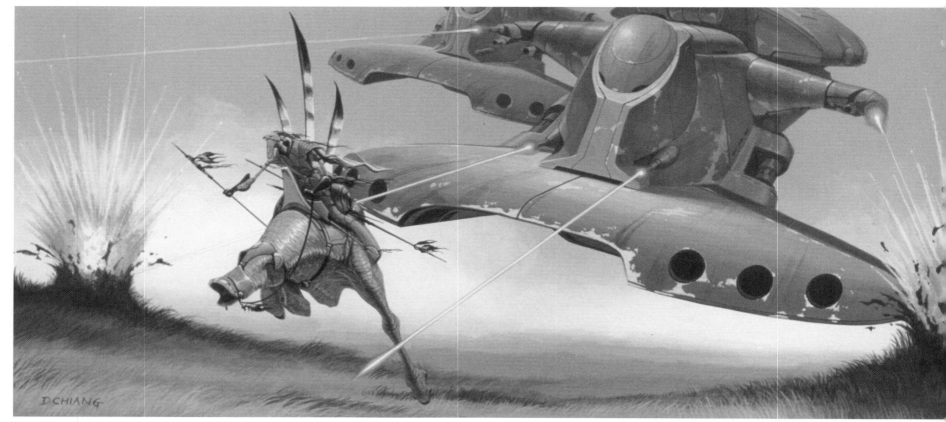

AN ARMORED ASSAULT TANK CHASING A GUNGAN ON A KAADU,
CONCEPT PAINTING BY DOUG CHIANG.

AN ARMORED ASSAULT TANK IN ACTION, *STAR WARS*: EPISODE I *THE PHANTOM MENACE* (1999).

02 | ARMORED
ASSAULT TANK (AAT)

FIRST APPEARANCE :
Star Wars: Episode I *The Phantom Menace* (1999)

DIFFICULTY :

DESIGN MANUFACTURER:	MAXIMUM SPEED:	LENGTH:	CREW:
Baktoid Armor Workshop	55 kph (35 mph)	9.75 m (32 ft)	4 battle droids (commander, pilot & 2 gunners)

DURING THE FINAL BATTLE SCENE IN *THE PHANTOM MENACE*, IN CONTRAST TO THE PEACEFUL GREENERY OF THE NABOO LANDSCAPE, SWARMS OF MALEVOLENT AATS DESCEND UPON THE GUNGAN ARMIES.

The brutish design evokes a sense of power, a warning to civilians that, despite its slow and arduous approach, they should take heed and clear the path.

The majority of the vehicles in Episode I were created using CGI technology and only a few key ships were actually built. One such vehicle was the Trade Federation tank which was constructed full-size for use during the Theed Plaza scenes.

Again the production design for *The Phantom Menace* defies what we're used to seeing in science-fiction. They're neither futuristic, nor antiquated. Design director Doug Chiang created the initial concept. During an interview for *The Beginning*, a documentary about the making of Episode I, Chiang reveals, "The magic of designing for film is that you are not bound by reality." You can see how he takes advantage of this perspective given that despite its obvious weight, the tank floats several feet off the ground.

The design was evolved by Fred Hole, who had previously worked on *Star Wars:* Episode VI *Return of the Jedi*. The prop was raised from the ground by two caster wheels in addition to a monopole with a wheel supporting the large overhanging turret at the back. This meant it could be conveniently positioned around set. Luckily, it was mostly built using polystyrene foam, meaning it was not quite as heavy as it would have been in the *Star Wars* galaxy.

Like podracers, the tanks use repulsorlift technology, allowing them to float above the ground. Despite its heavy and sedentary appearance, it is always ready to strike. The Trade Federation created its army and vehicles in secret under the influence of the mysterious Darth Sidious. AATs were built by the Baktoid Armor Workshop and designed to be the key player on the frontline of droid invasions. Its distinctive "foot" is made almost entirely of solid plate armor, enabling it to plough through any obstructions. AATs are laden with heavy artillery designed to mow down any opposing forces. The tank carries a crew of four battle droids: a pilot, two gunners, and a commander.

02

ARMORED
ASSAULT TANK
(AAT)

<table>
<tr><td>**CUTTING TIPS**</td><td></td></tr>
</table>

CUTTING TIPS

Cut and score the template as per the guide section at the beginning of the book. Start by cutting out the smaller details such as the clouds and panelling details on the tank.

FOLDING TIPS

1

With the printed side facing you, hold the model upside down and *lever fold* the main *horizon fold*.

2

With the model still in this position, *push out* the *valley folds* that connect the front "foot" of the tank to the *background plate*.

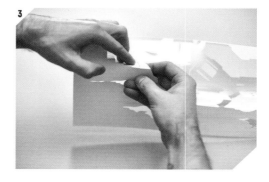

3

Work your way around the *valley folds*, holding the paper in one hand and pushing the fold using fingers of your other hand.

4

Turn the model over to the non-printed side and gradually work around the *mountain folds*. For example, hold the body of the model as shown and push back the paper along the fold.

5

Use a *skewer* to fold the small *mountain fold* on the front part of the foot.

6

Once the model has been folded flat and reopened, push back the flap at the rear to an angle of around 45°.

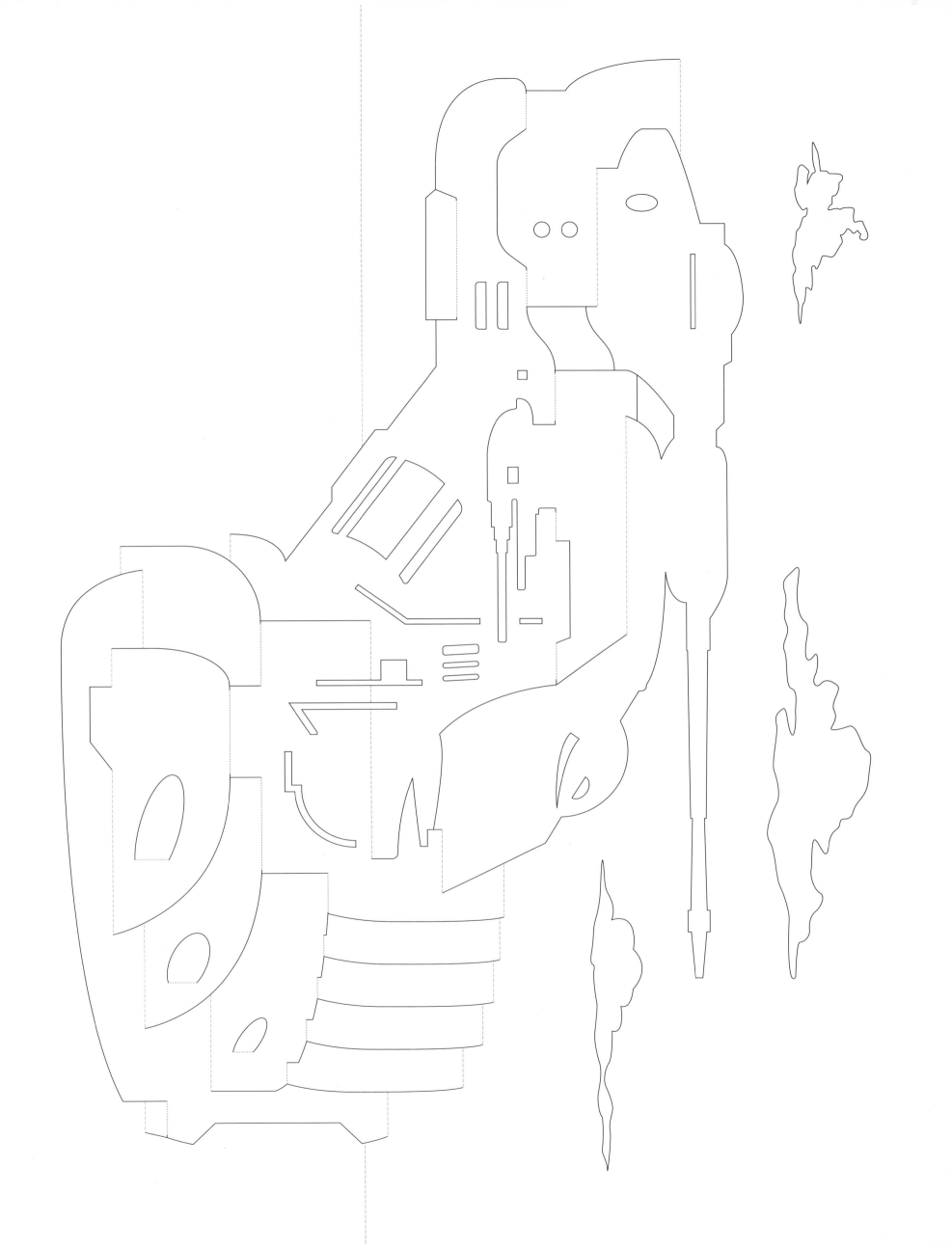

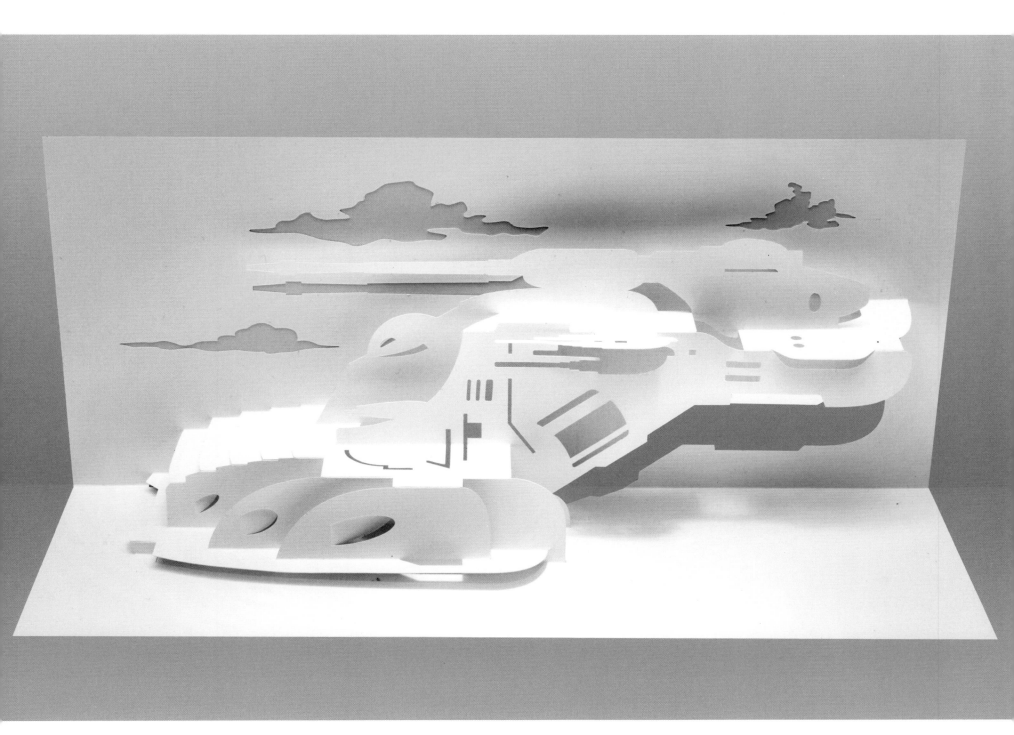

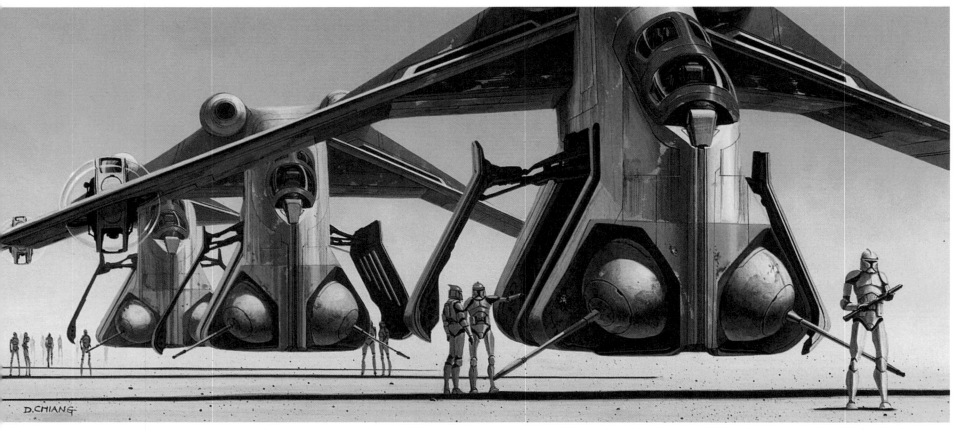

REPUBLIC ATTACK GUNSHIPS, CONCEPT PAINTING BY DOUG CHIANG.

TRANSPORT ATTACKING GEONOSIS, CONCEPT ART BY ERIK TIEMENS.

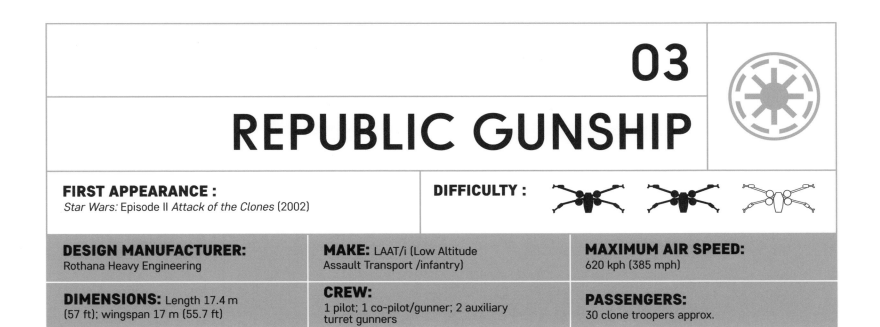

03

REPUBLIC GUNSHIP

FIRST APPEARANCE :
Star Wars: Episode II *Attack of the Clones* (2002)

DIFFICULTY :

DESIGN MANUFACTURER: Rothana Heavy Engineering	**MAKE:** LAAT/i (Low Altitude Assault Transport /infantry)
DIMENSIONS: Length 17.4 m (57 ft); wingspan 17 m (55.7 ft)	**CREW:** 1 pilot; 1 co-pilot/gunner; 2 auxiliary turret gunners

MAXIMUM AIR SPEED: 620 kph (385 mph)

PASSENGERS: 30 clone troopers approx.

IN THE PETRANAKI ARENA ON GEONOSIS, THE JEDI ARE STRUGGLING AGAINST COUNT DOOKU'S DROID ARMY. WITH EVERY PASSING MOMENT THE OUTLOOK BECOMES BLEAKER AS WAVE AFTER WAVE OF DROIDS OVERWHELM OUR HEROES.

Just as it seems the Jedi will fall, Master Yoda miraculously arrives aboard a Republic gunship accompanied by a squadron of clone troopers. The Republic gunship, also known as LAAT/i (which stands for Low Altitude Assault Transport/infantry) is one of the most widely used ships during the Clone Wars.

After receiving concept paintings of the ship by Doug Chiang, John Goodson, the lead concept model maker, was immediately inspired by scenes from the war movie *Apocalypse Now*. We can see this is heavily reflected in the design. In particular the LAAT/i directly references Russian military helicopters, especially the MI-24 Hind, with its dual "hunchback" cockpit and open sides for quick deployment of troops.

It wasn't just real-world vehicles that aided Goodson in the development of the design. During his research phase, he recalled the mechanical flaps at the rear of the T-47 snowspeeder from *The Empire Strikes Back*, remembering how they aided braking. Goodson was inspired by this mechanism and evolved it for use in

the LAAT/i. When the ship's side doors slide open, they provide a secondary function by flaring outward to help it reduce speed as it comes into a landing.

The addition of the clear bubble turret at the side was a late suggestion from George Lucas. Goodson remarked that its design was intended to mimic a mini Death Star.

A fully detailed and painted scale model was built for the sign-off process. However, every appearance the gunship made during *Attack of the Clones* was purely CGI.

The LAAT/i was designed to transport thirty clone troopers alongside a pilot and primary gunner. Two ancillary troopers wield the side turrets that swing out from the main cargo area. Designed and built by Rothana Heavy Engineering, they are capable of reaching speeds of up to 620 kilometers (385 miles) per hour. Aside from transporting clones, the vehicles provide another primary function as Republic escorts.

03
—
REPUBLIC GUNSHIP

CUTTING TIPS

Cut and score the template as per the guide section at the beginning of the book. Start by cutting out the smaller details such as the clouds, panelling details, and windows on the ship. Try to remove every window.

FOLDING TIPS

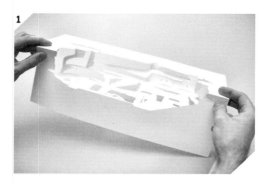

With the printed side facing you, *lever fold* the main horizon *valley fold*, then push out the three folds at the base of the ship.

Rotate the paper 180° and *push out* all of the *valley folds* connected to the background plate.

Work your way around the remaining *valley folds* in the center of the model.

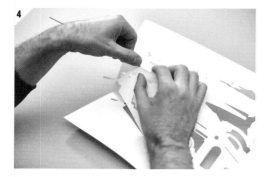

Turn the model over to the non-printed side and gradually work around the *mountain folds*. Normally the *pinch* approach will work but use a *skewer* for tighter spaces.

Form the wing by holding the body of the ship in one hand (use the space where the side opening of the ship is) and in the other hand push the wing upward.

Once the model has been folded flat and reopened, fold out the turret on the wing and the side turret so they are at 90° to the main ship.

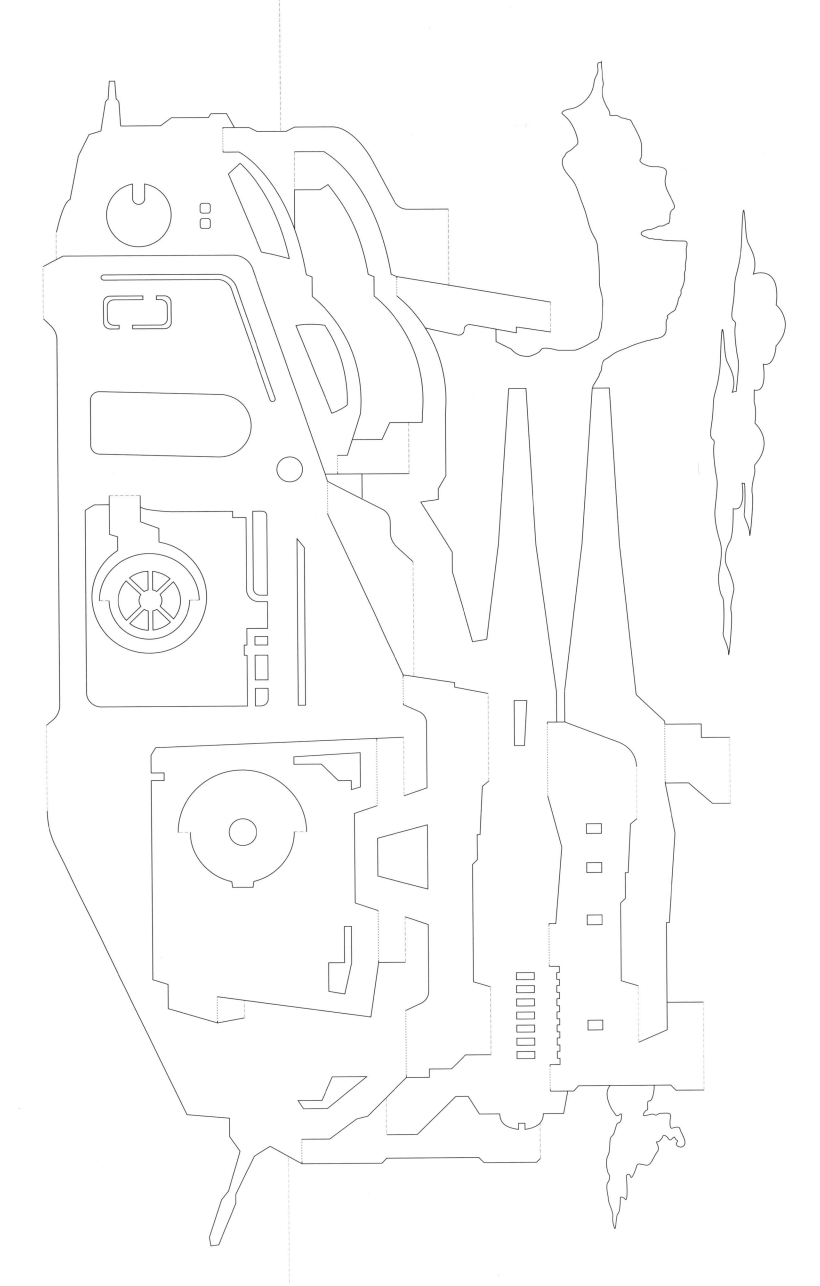

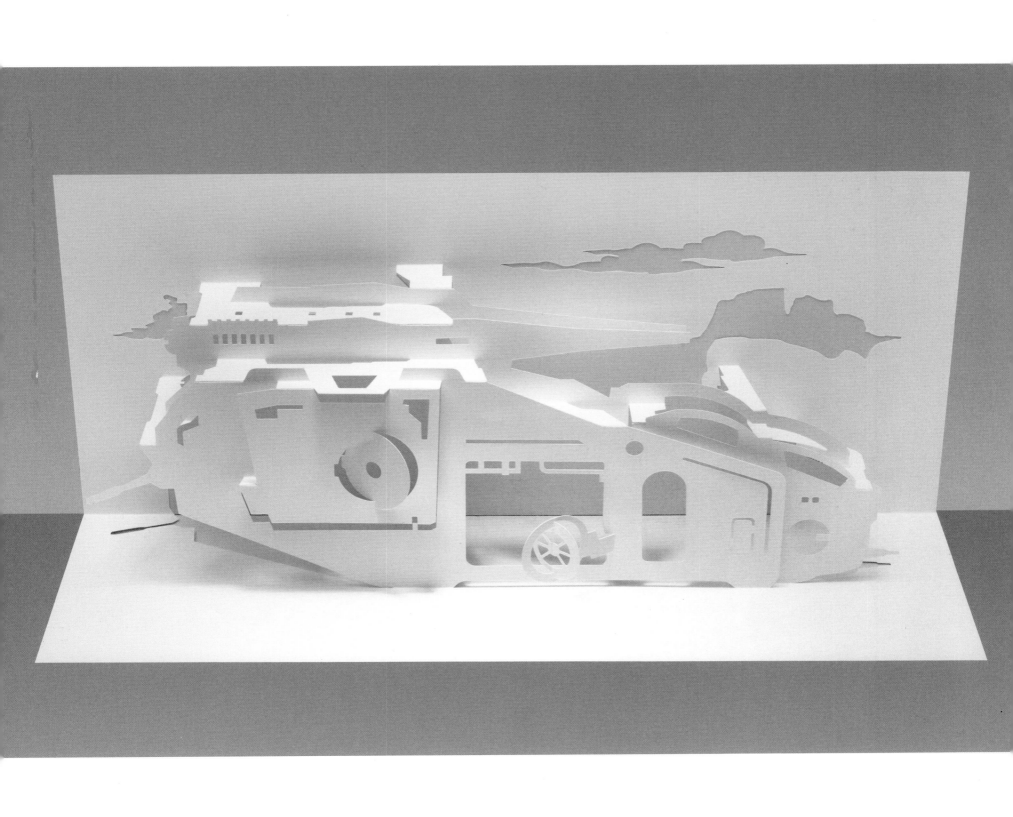

THE BATTLE OF GEONOSIS, AN AT-TE SURROUNDED BY CLONE TROOPERS,
STAR WARS: EPISODE II *ATTACK OF THE CLONES* (2002).

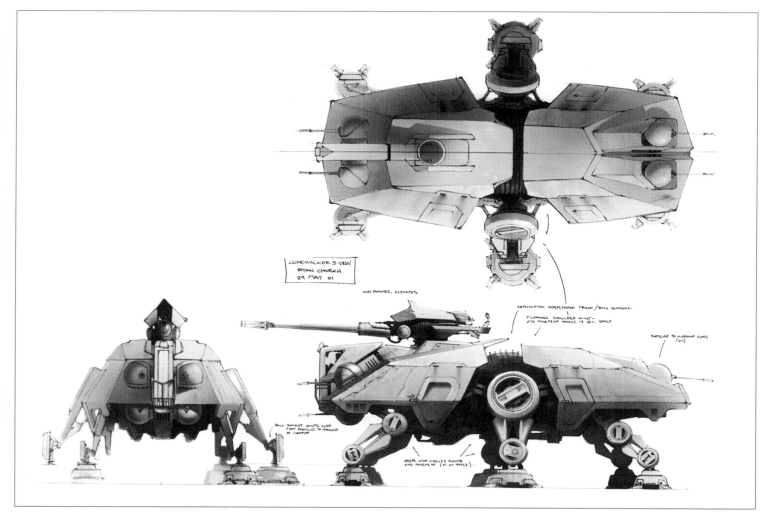

THE AT-TE (PREVIOUSLY NAMED CLONEWALKER), CONCEPT ART BY RYAN CHURCH.

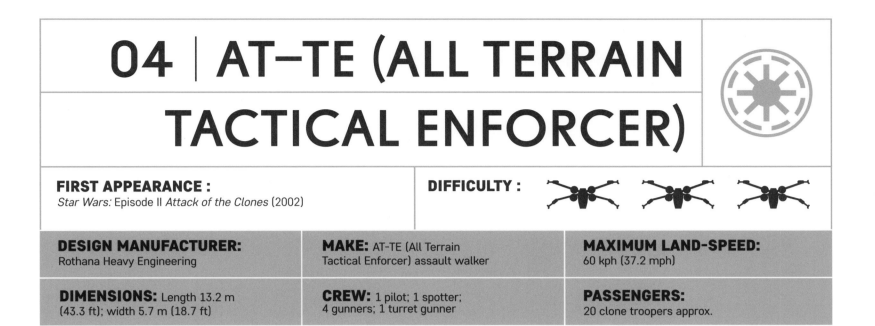

04 | AT-TE (ALL TERRAIN TACTICAL ENFORCER)

FIRST APPEARANCE :
Star Wars: Episode II *Attack of the Clones* (2002)

DIFFICULTY :

DESIGN MANUFACTURER: Rothana Heavy Engineering	**MAKE:** AT-TE (All Terrain Tactical Enforcer) assault walker	**MAXIMUM LAND-SPEED:** 60 kph (37.2 mph)
DIMENSIONS: Length 13.2 m (43.3 ft); width 5.7 m (18.7 ft)	**CREW:** 1 pilot; 1 spotter; 4 gunners; 1 turret gunner	**PASSENGERS:** 20 clone troopers approx.

AT-TES INEVITABLY DRAW COMPARISON WITH THE AT-ATS WE SEE IN *THE EMPIRE STRIKES BACK* AND *RETURN OF THE JEDI*. DURING THE CLONE WARS IT'S THE FIRST TIME WE SEE WALKER TECHNOLOGY BEING USED.

Outside of the *Star Wars* fiction, vehicles such as these are important to establish the length of time the entire saga is spread over. Just like how we can compare the latest model of a car manufacturer with its twenty-year-old predecessor, there will be noticeable similarities but obvious physical changes. I was a casual reader of the *Expanded Universe* (now *Legends*) and while I enjoyed the plot, as a visually led person, I needed to see it in order to understand the timescale. The most important part of the prequel trilogy for me is the beauty of the aesthetic evolution led by Doug Chiang.

No scale models were produced of the AT-TE. During the three years between Episodes I and II, ILM had vastly improved abilities in digital and Lucas was keen to push them to their limits by creating entirely CGI battle scenes.

The armor of AT-TEs alludes to a hybrid technological creature, splicing the DNA of a giant Atlas beetle, a slow and determined stride, with the strength of a rhinoceros. Unphased by the pandemonium that lies ahead, one of its primary roles as a transporter is to carry up to twenty clone troopers across a variety of unforgiving landscapes. Its six legs enable it to tackle steep hills, rugged terrains, and not to mention ploughing through enemy troops, all with great ease. Enemy mines hidden in the ground prove to be no obstacle either.

Built by Rothana Heavy Engineering, AT-TEs were also designed to be carried by LAAT/c gunships. Their sturdy bodies allow them to be dropped from a considerable height onto a battlefield. Combing these features with a huge missile launcher and six laser cannons, AT-TEs are a force to be reckoned with.

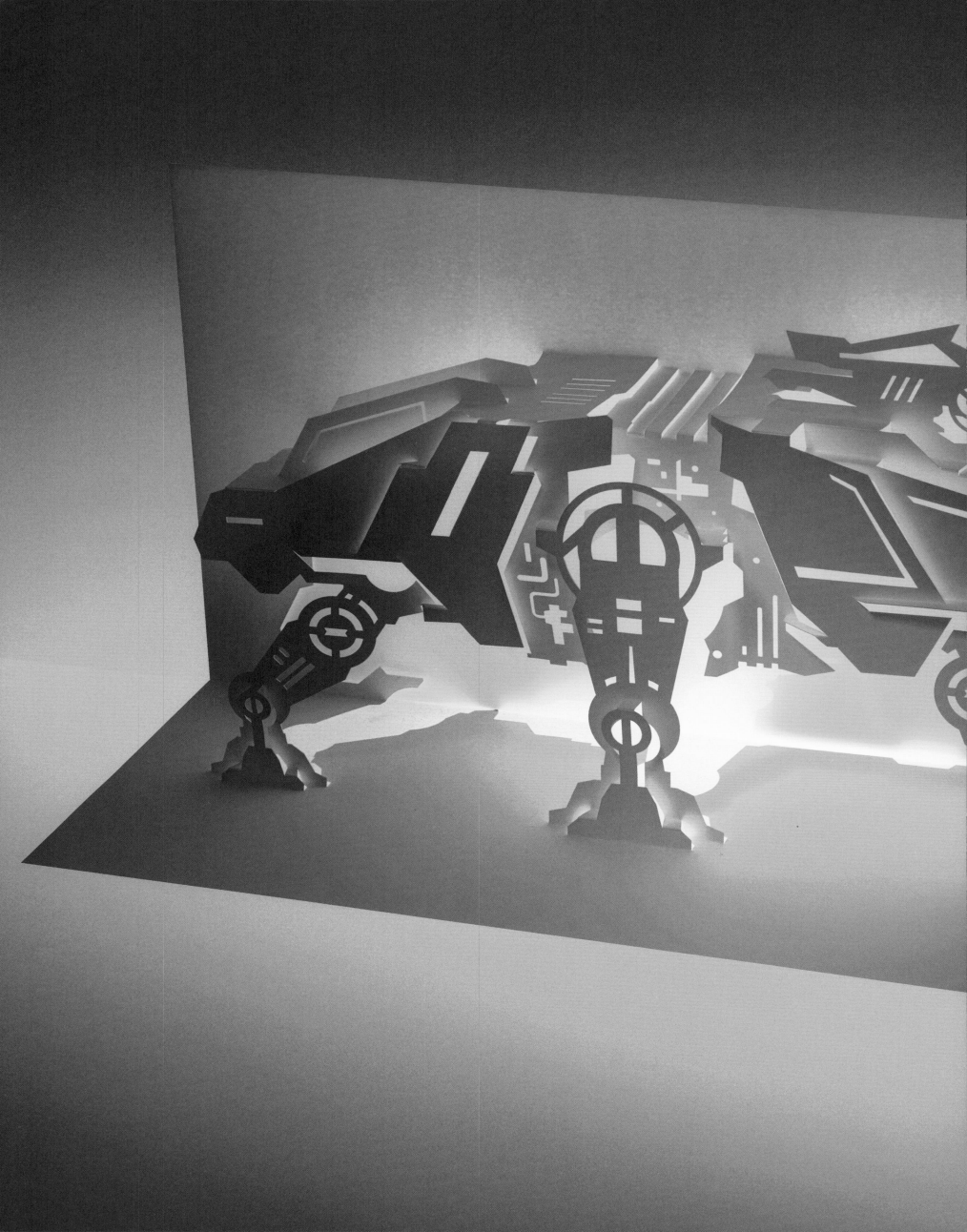

04

—

AT-TE
(ALL TERRAIN
TACTICAL ENFORCER)

CUTTING TIPS

Cut and score the template as per the guide section at the beginning of the book. Start by cutting out the smaller details such as the panelling details on the main armor and legs.

FOLDING TIPS

1

With the printed side facing you, *lever fold* the main *horizon valley*.

2

Push out the *valley folds* at the base of the three legs. At the same time alternate between the *mountain folds* that form the protruding section of the foot. Use a *skewer* for these tight folds.

3

With the printed side facing you, push out the *valley folds* that connect the tops of the model to the *background plate*.

4

Work on the remaining *valley folds* within the body of the vehicle.

5

Turn the model over to the non-printed side and use the *lever fold* approach to crease the *mountain folds* on the outer sides of the vehicle. *Push out* the remaining *mountain folds* within the main body.

6

Fold the model flat by working it from behind. Pay special attention to the legs ensuring they don't buckle and crease incorrectly.

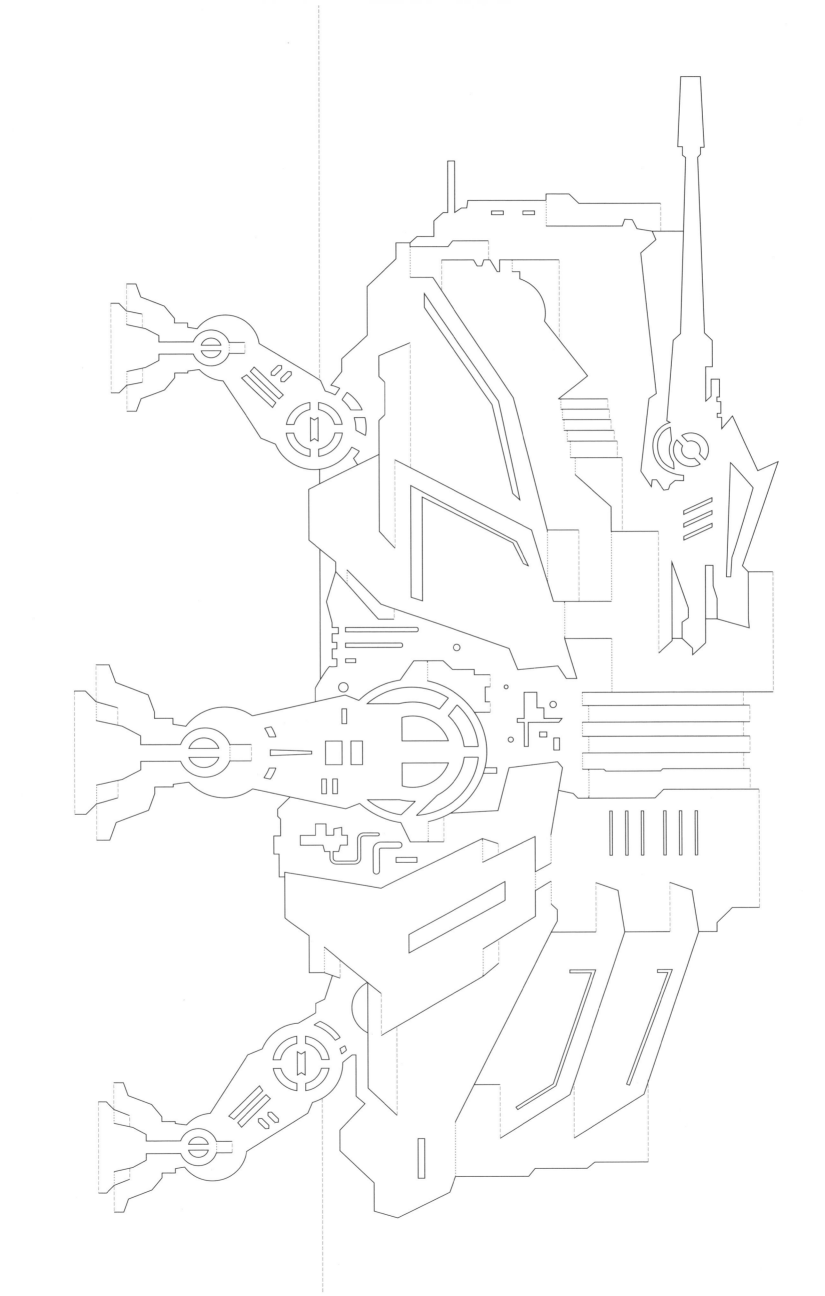

THE JEDI FIGHTER WITH WINGS OPENED AND CLOSED,
CONCEPT ART BY RYAN CHURCH.

ANAKIN AND OBI-WAN'S JEDI FIGHTERS SURROUNDED BY ARC-170
FIGHTERS, *STAR WARS:* EPISODE III *REVENGE OF THE SITH* (2005).

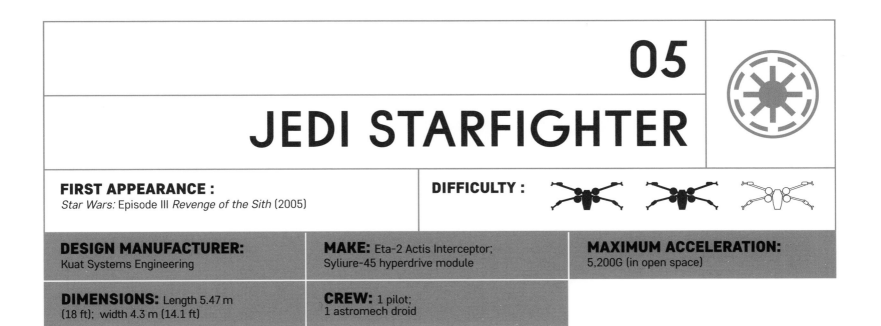

JEDI STARFIGHTER

FIRST APPEARANCE :
Star Wars: Episode III *Revenge of the Sith* (2005)

DIFFICULTY :

DESIGN MANUFACTURER:
Kuat Systems Engineering

MAKE: Eta-2 Actis Interceptor;
Syliure-45 hyperdrive module

MAXIMUM ACCELERATION:
5,200G (in open space)

DIMENSIONS: Length 5.47 m
(18 ft); width 4.3 m (14.1 ft)

CREW: 1 pilot;
1 astromech droid

DURING A SEEMINGLY PEACEFUL START TO *THE REVENGE OF THE SITH*, TWO JEDI STARFIGHTERS GLIDE OVER A REPUBLIC STARSHIP BEFORE PLUMMETING INTO THE CHAOTIC BATTLE OF CORUSCANT BELOW.

An early triangular version of a Jedi starfighter (or interceptor) piloted by Obi-Wan was introduced in Episode II but for the third film in the trilogy, the design had significantly evolved—inspired by a relatively unusual influence. As part of the marketing for Episode II, a toy version of the original starfighter was produced. As with most toys, the manufacturers like to add additional features in order to increase playability. John Goodson, as concept model maker, saw how the original Jedi interceptor toy had extra hidden features and articulation points to the wings. He was so impressed with these additions that he wanted to incorporate them into the new design. A variety of concept drawings by Ryan Church demonstrating the new folding S-foils were presented to George Lucas and while impressed with the new design, Lucas suggested introducing the unmistakable octagonal TIE fighter window to the cockpit. At this point, it was clear that the starfighter would become a poster child piece that illustrates how the design aesthetics from Episode III would carry over to the original trilogy, set nearly twenty years later. From a personal standpoint, it plays a small but significant role in showing how the entire Republic armada would be commandeered by the newly formed Empire— therefore it's entirely plausible and important to see how visual styles were inherited, too.

In addition to the cockpit window, sheeting similar to the solar panel of a regular TIE was added to the underside of the wing fins, that once opened out share an undeniable similarity to the profile of the future Empire's signature fighter.

A final design change from Lucas was the incorporation of a plug-in astromech droid as co-pilot. Given the apparent thinness of the wings, this would be physically impossible. Shouldn't the lower half of the astromech be visible from the underside of the wings? Technically yes, but with some convenient camera angles, digital editing, and of course, cutting a little bit of slack, this wasn't a problem.

A single life-size fighter was built for filming close-up shots and during production was repainted with several different schemes so it could serve as several different ships—one for Anakin, Obi-Wan, and Plo Koon.

Manufactured by Kuat Systems Engineering, this Eta-2 model was designed with the Jedi's Force-assisted abilities in mind. The absence of heavy instruments and shields means that even the smallest superficial damage would spell certain death. However, the small and light construction of the craft enables agile combat enhanced by the quick reactions of a skilled Jedi pilot.

05
—
JEDI
STARFIGHTER

CUTTING TIPS

Cut and score the template as per the guide section at the beginning of the book. Start by cutting out the smaller details such as the octagonal window frame, panel details, and stars.

FOLDING TIPS

1. With the printed side facing you, hold the template upside down and *push out* all the *valley folds* on the *background plate* including the main horizon.

2. *Push out* the *valley fold* that connects the base of the ship to the *base plate* of the model—not forgetting the *valley fold* just under the cockpit window.

3. Turn the model to the non-printed side. Hold the main body of the ship flat on a surface with one hand; in the other, pull the cockpit forward. If the *mountain folds* have been half-cut properly the model will begin to stand up.

4. In a similar process as before, hold the hull of the model in one hand and using the finger and thumb of the other, twist the octagonal window away from you.

5. The final steps are to position the non-structural elements of the model. Fold the outer part of the wings under the model as illustrated and position the upper section at an angle of around 45°. Tip the astromech upright.

6. Finally, fold the sides of the cockpit window down and then rest the two small tabs over the edge of the octagonal window to keep it in position.

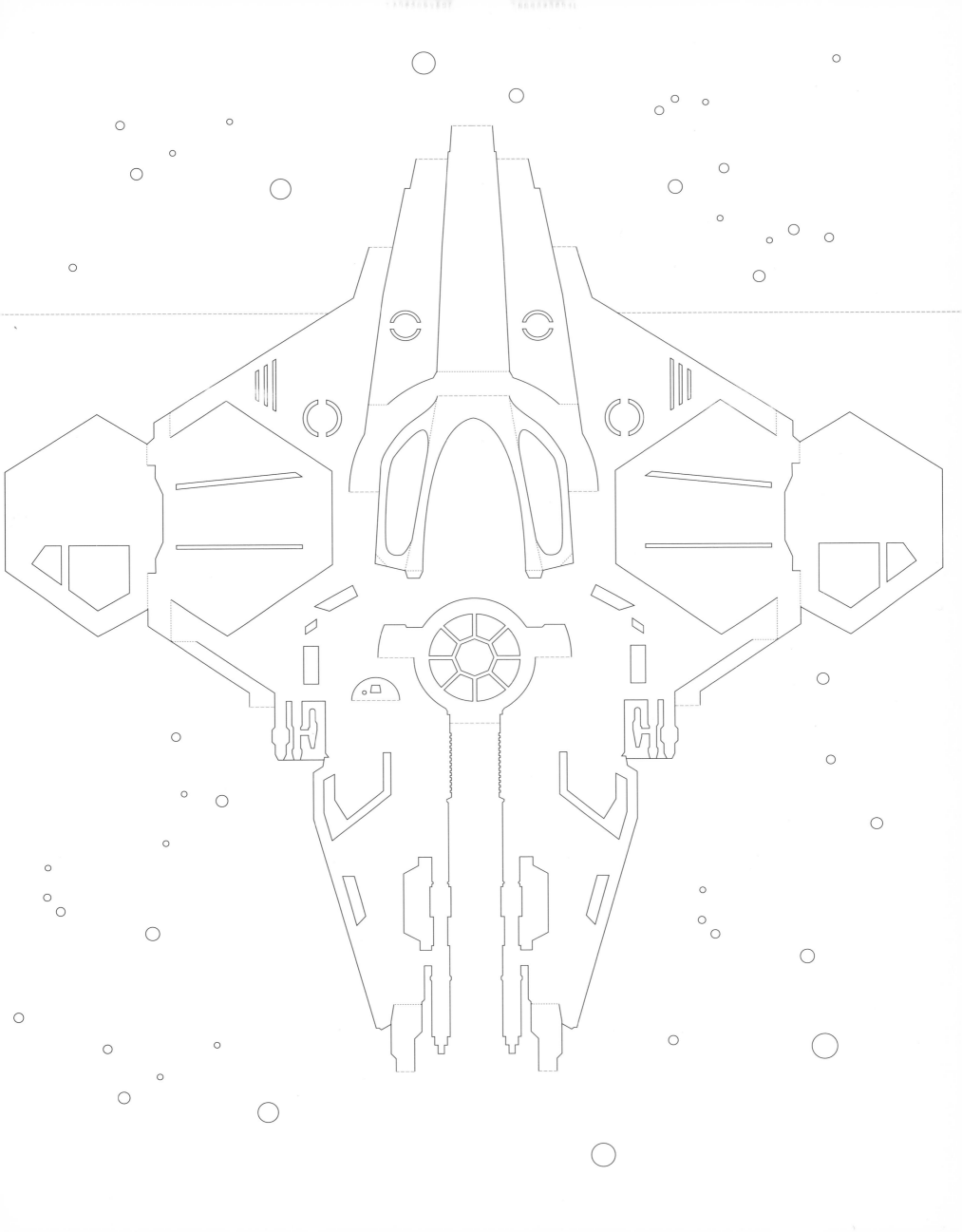

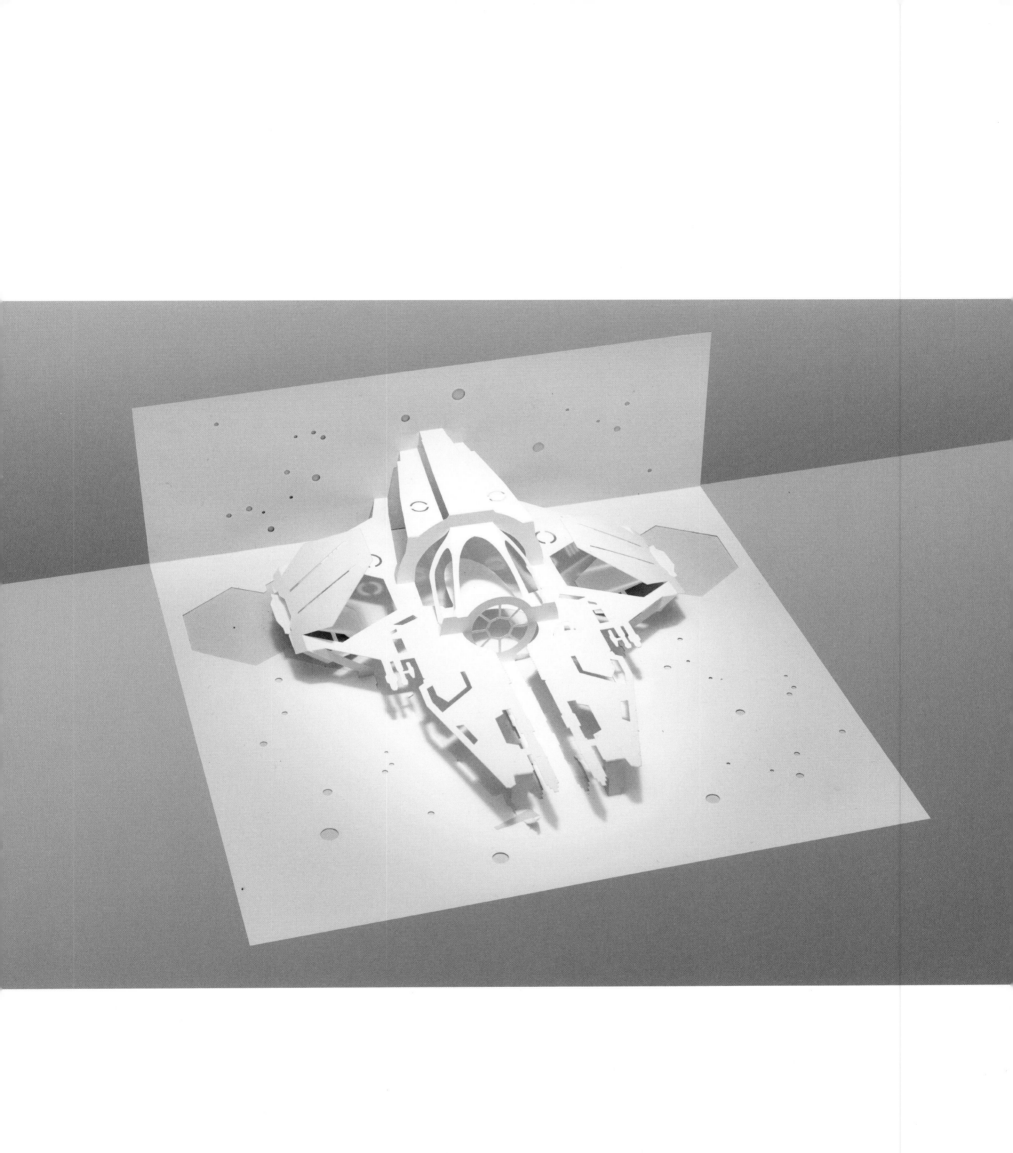

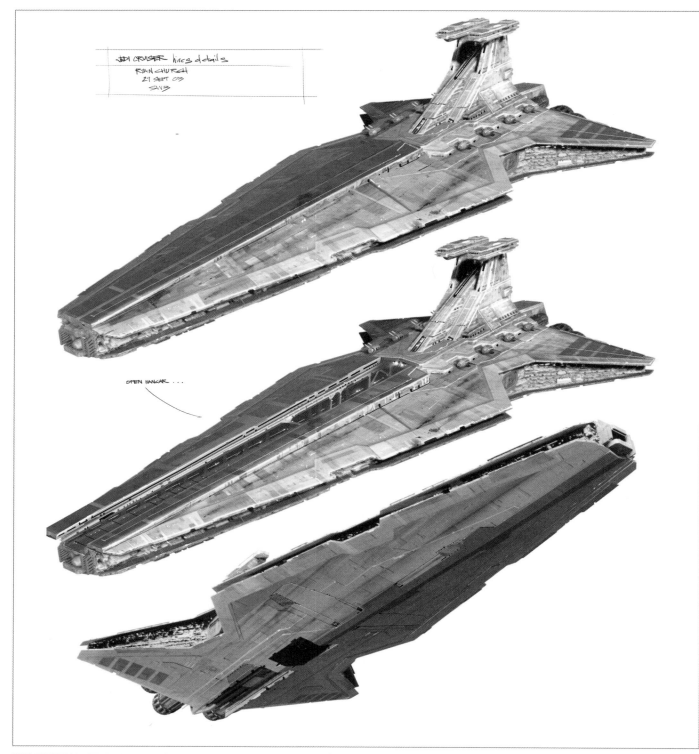

THE REPUBLIC ATTACK CRUISER (PREVIOUSLY NAMED JEDI CRUISER),
CONCEPT ART BY RYAN CHURCH.

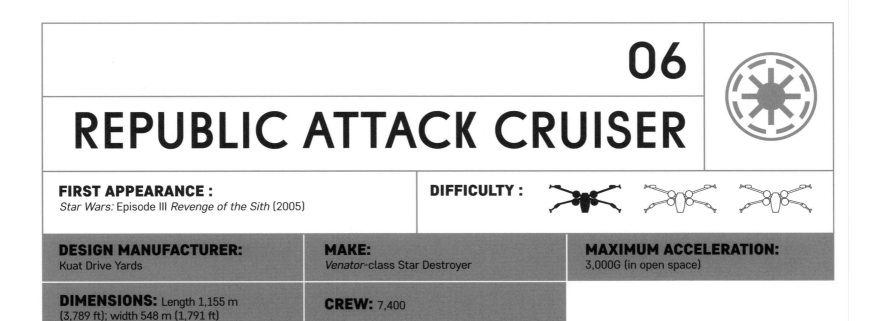

REPUBLIC ATTACK CRUISER

06

FIRST APPEARANCE :
Star Wars: Episode III *Revenge of the Sith* (2005)

DIFFICULTY :

DESIGN MANUFACTURER: Kuat Drive Yards	**MAKE:** *Venator*-class Star Destroyer	**MAXIMUM ACCELERATION:** 3,000G (in open space)
DIMENSIONS: Length 1,155 m (3,789 ft); width 548 m (1,791 ft)	**CREW:** 7,400	

IN THE OPENING MOMENTS OF *REVENGE OF THE SITH*, ANAKIN AND OBI-WAN APPEAR, ROVING IN THEIR JEDI INTERCEPTORS MEANDERING THROUGH SPACE BEFORE CRUISING OVER THE COLOSSAL *VENATOR*-CLASS REPUBLIC ATTACK CRUISER.

In these final times before the hijacking of the Galactic Republic by Supreme Chancellor Palpatine, the huge wedge-shaped spacecraft already bears a resemblance to the Imperial Star Destroyers that would appear in the future (via the original trilogy). As before with the Jedi starfighter, which bears the unmistakable TIE fighter window design, we can see how the production designers for Episode III alluded to the passage of time. By creating vehicles that were not identical yet borrowed features, embellishments, or shapes, we begin to understand how technology was to evolve over the next nineteen years. I like to imagine the famous graphic depicting a monkey on all fours that within several steps transforms into a Neanderthal and then onward into modern-day man. Where does the *Venator*-class sit on this linear progression? How many more iterations of the ship appeared before we reach the likes of Star Destroyers and, of course, ultimately Kylo Ren's personal ship, ominously named the *Finalizer*?

I love the design of this ship for its contrast to the Imperial Star Destroyer. At first glance they are strikingly similar. However, the *Venator* portrays a "softer" style with notched recesses along the side and the dual towers of the bridge are almost like insect antennas. This gives the ship a lifelike character in comparison to its successor. I was sure to include these features in the kirigami version. Perhaps this was a deliberate choice in alluding that the *Venator* came from a more peaceful and democratic era in the galaxy.

Republic attack cruisers were first deployed during the Clone Wars. Manufactured by the Kuat Drive Yards, the early incarnation of an *Imperial*-class Star Destroyer was commissioned to helm the frontlines in the war against the Separatists. Capable of carrying over 420 starfighters, 40 gunships and 24 AT-TEs, they ensured that the might of the Republic would prevail, paving the way for Palpatine's meticulous and devious plot to become Emperor.

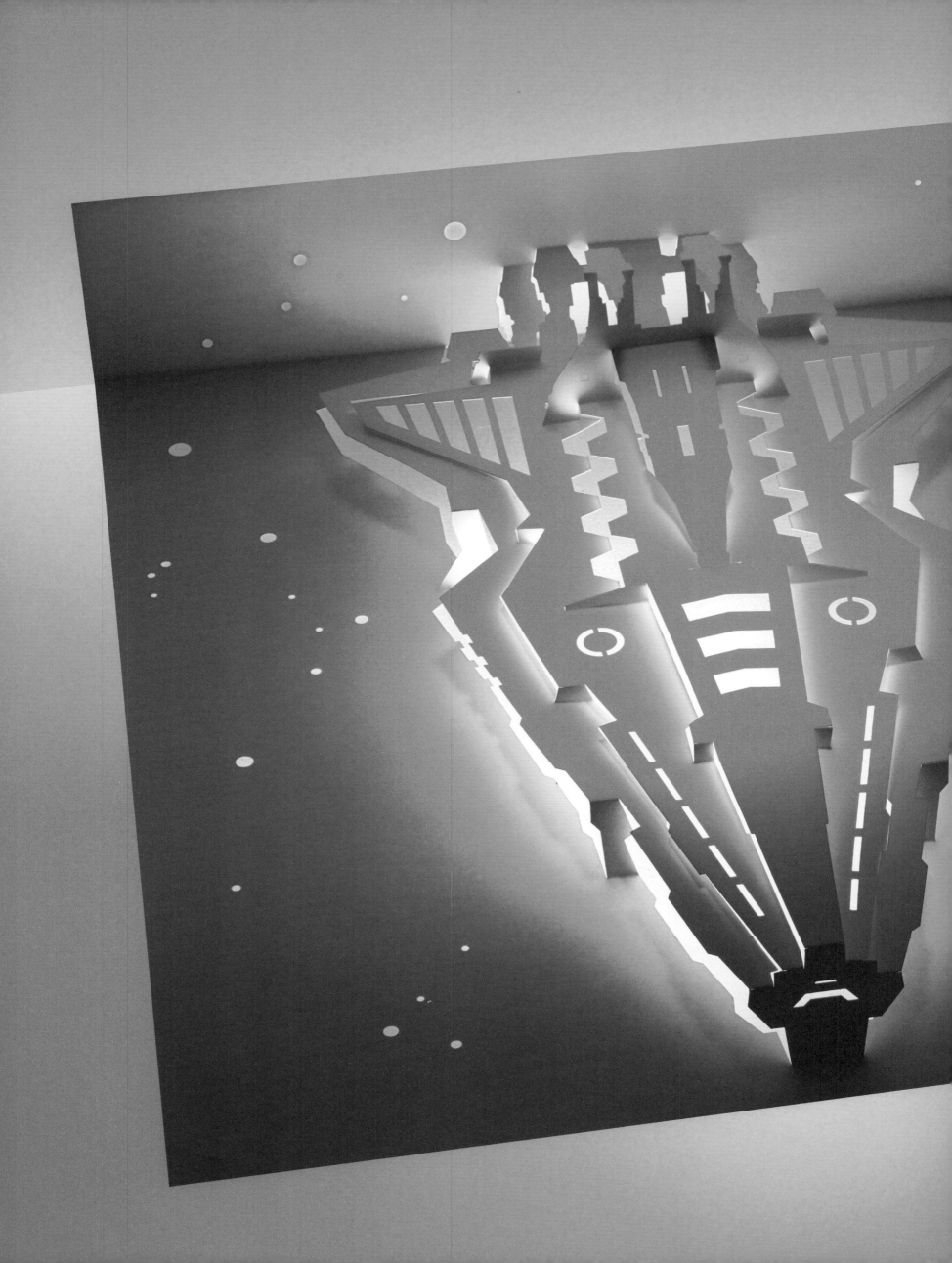

06

—

REPUBLIC ATTACK CRUISER

CUTTING TIPS	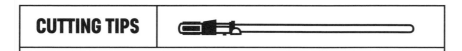

Cut and score the template as per the guide section at the beginning of the book. Start by cutting out the smaller details such as the stars, panelling details and, not forgetting about the tiny slot near the center of the page.

FOLDING TIPS

With the printed side facing you *push out* all the *valley folds* on the *background plate,* including the main *horizon*.

Push out the *valley folds* that are the struts which raise the ship off the *base plate*. Their opposing *mountain folds* should begin to crease if they have been half-cut properly.

Pinch the tip of ship along the *mountain folds*.

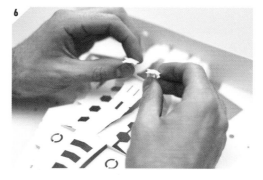

The majority of the remaining folds can be completed by holding various lengths of the ship in one hand and pulling the upper lengths toward you with the other hand.

Fold the ship flat to complete the creases. Once it is open and positioned correctly, place the tip of the upper deck into the slot so that it creates a sloping section.

Tip back the *mountain folds* of the two bridges so they are 90° to the towers.

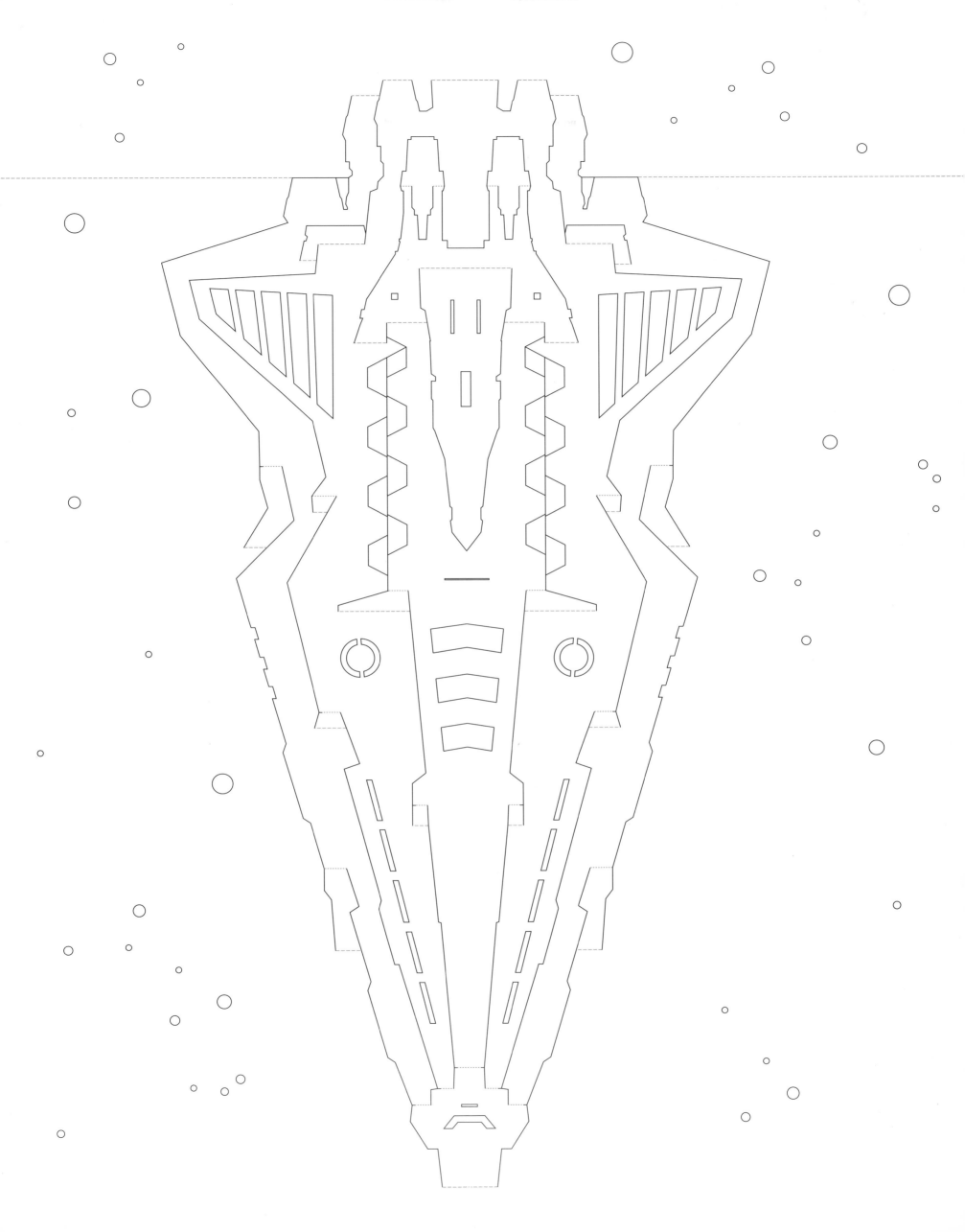

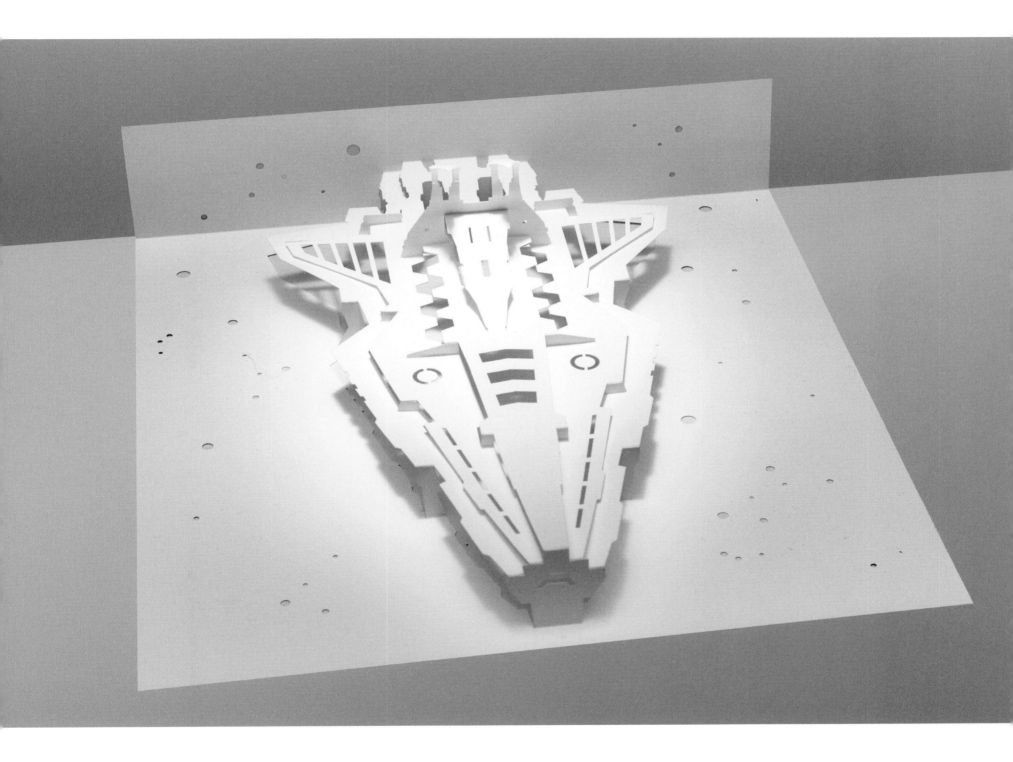

MOS EISLEY, CONCEPT ART BY RALPH MCQUARRIE, 1975.

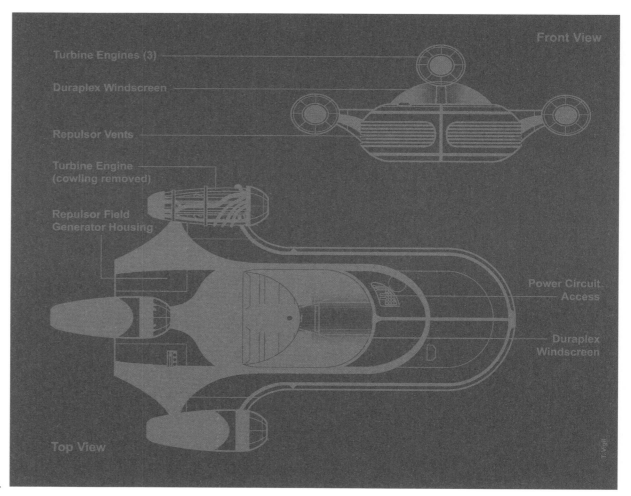

SCHEMATIC OF LUKE'S LANDSPEEDER.

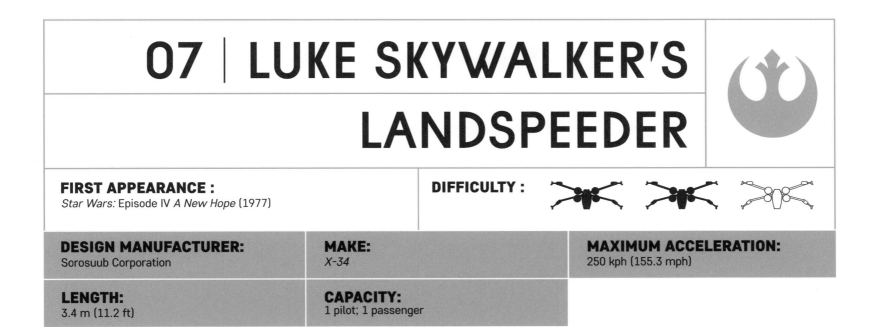

07 | LUKE SKYWALKER'S LANDSPEEDER

FIRST APPEARANCE :
Star Wars: Episode IV *A New Hope* (1977)

DIFFICULTY :

DESIGN MANUFACTURER:	MAKE:	MAXIMUM ACCELERATION:
Sorosuub Corporation	X-34	250 kph (155.3 mph)

LENGTH:	CAPACITY:
3.4 m (11.2 ft)	1 pilot; 1 passenger

THE GENIUS OF *STAR WARS:* EPISODE IV *A NEW HOPE* SPANS FAR BEYOND THE MAIN PLOTLINE. PART OF ITS SUCCESS WAS THE CREATION A THOROUGHLY DEVELOPED WORLD.

Every scene, costume, and vehicle was densely packed with details, meaning that within a few frames we were transported to an utterly convincing otherworld. For me, one relatively inconspicuous aspect multiplied its ability to do that to no end— rust, dirt, and dents. Audiences in the 1970s had become so accustomed to streamlined metallic ships as representations of advanced technology, that when they first laid eyes on the battered, and paradoxically outdated, technology used in *Star Wars*, they were transfixed. Even though the saga occurred in a distant galaxy long ago, we are also aware that technologically the characters are advanced. It was this juxtaposition that made it so believable. Instead of being presented with smooth, clinical, and polished crafts, we got vehicles that have frankly seen better days. One such vehicle is Luke's landspeeder. Without knowing much about its history, the marvel of its appearance is that we know it had a history. The same applies to almost everything we see in *A New Hope,* especially on the oppressed civilian side.

Lucas drew inspiration from many sources for the landspeeder. In *The Making of Star Wars* he references resources such as comic books, sci-fi novels, and *National Geographic* magazines. After compiling his list, he tasked Ralph McQuarrie with creating a scene featuring the ship. Although the design went through several revisions, the final product is still very much anchored in the initial idea.

The life-size prop, of course, couldn't float a meter off the ground and instead was rested on a trio of wheels. The wheels were hidden by two long mirrors, angled just enough to reflect the ground giving the impression that it floated. To further enhance the effect, Vaseline was actually smeared on the lens to blur the area out! Many of these older techniques were replaced digitally during the various re-releases over the years. If you want to see the original versions you'll have to hunt down some old VHS copies.

Luke's landspeeder was his treasured possession. Despite its poor condition, it enabled him to visit his friends at the Tosche station, escaping the monotony of his daily farm chores. X-34s bear no weapons nor armor but have the ability to travel over even the roughest terrain with ease.

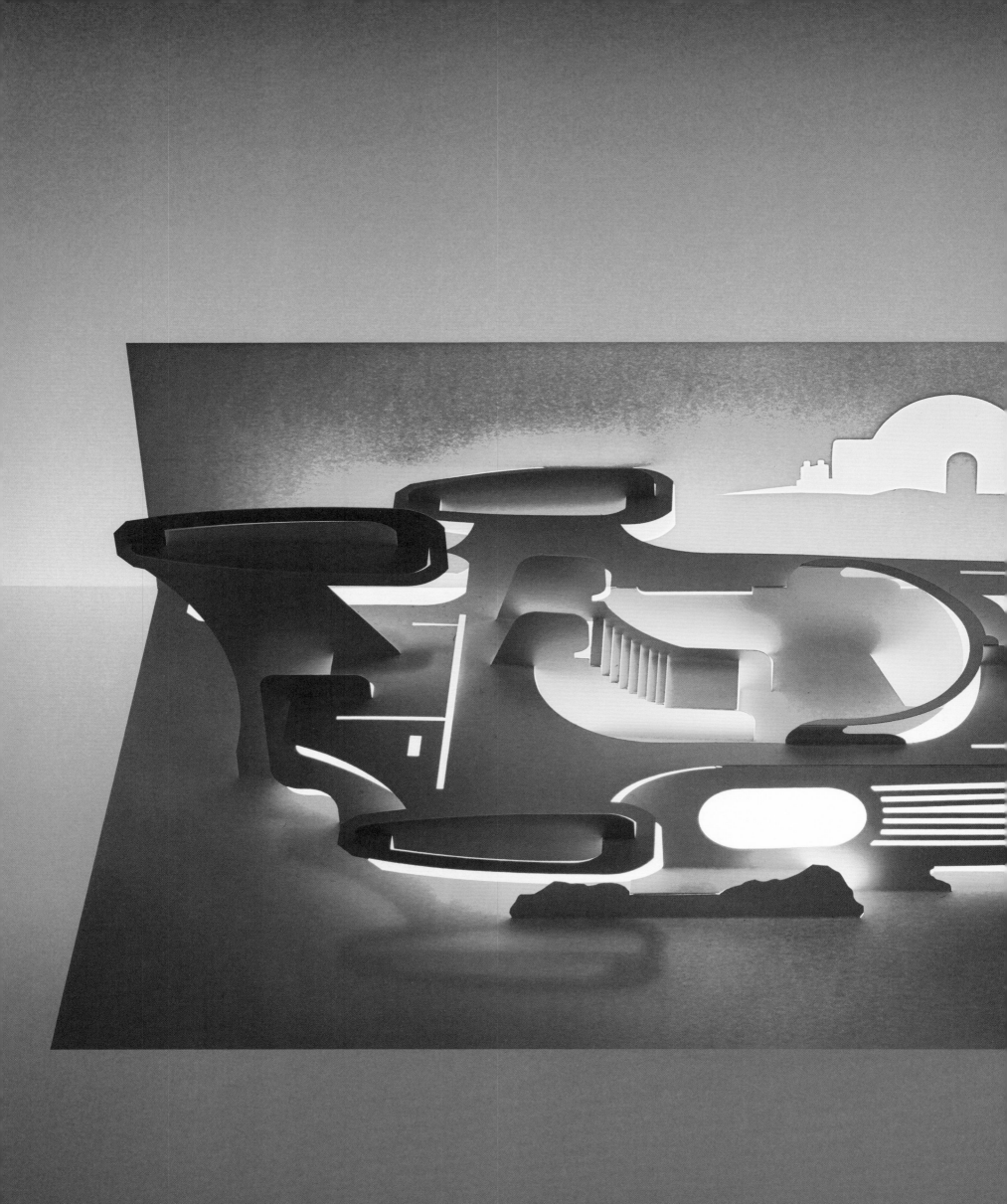

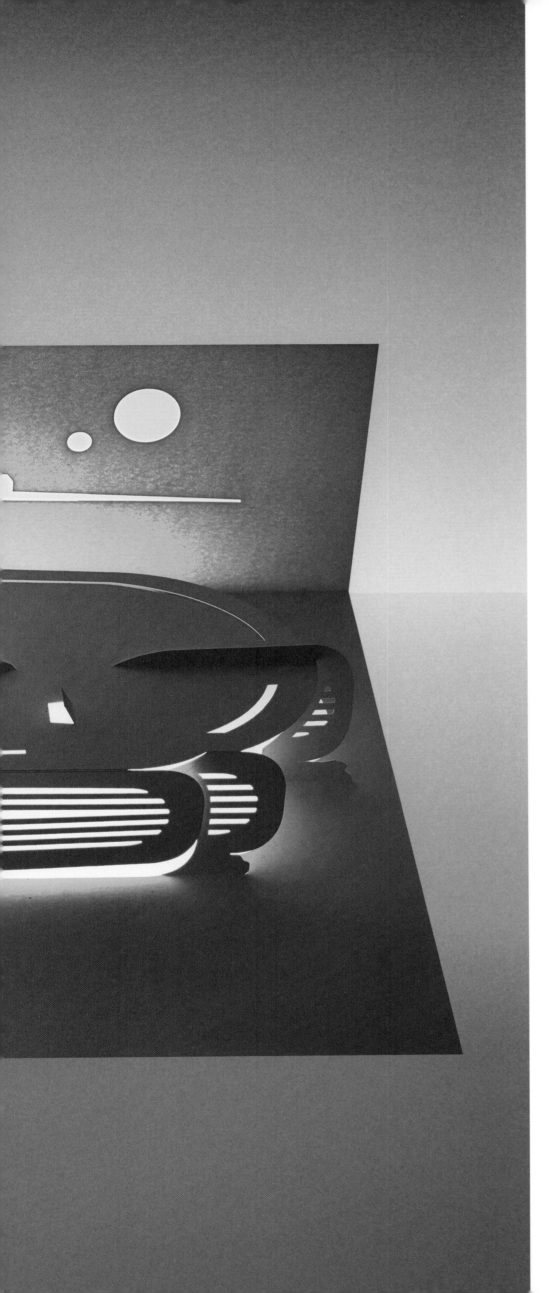

07
—
LUKE SKYWALKER'S LANDSPEEDER

CUTTING TIPS

Cut and score the template as per the guide section at the beginning of the book. Start by cutting out the inner details such as the farm building, twin suns, and grills on the side of the speeder.

FOLDING TIPS

1

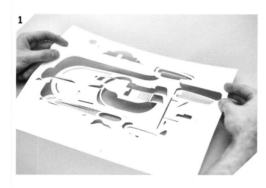

With the printed side facing you *lever fold* the main *horizon line* and then *push out* the *valley folds* at the base of the speeder.

2

Rotate the paper 180° and *push out* the single *valley fold* that connects the engine to the *background plane*.

3

Pinch together the small *valley* and *mountain folds* around the front of the speeder and the area that forms the windshield.

4

With one hand resting firmly on the *base plane*, use the other hand to pull the model toward you. The model should naturally stand up if it has been half-cut properly.

5

Using the headrest of the seat, you can invert the footwell part of the speeder.

6

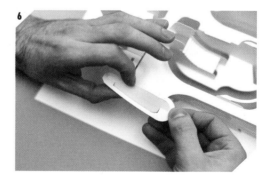

Finally, twist the folding sections of the three engines so they are perpendicular to their original state.

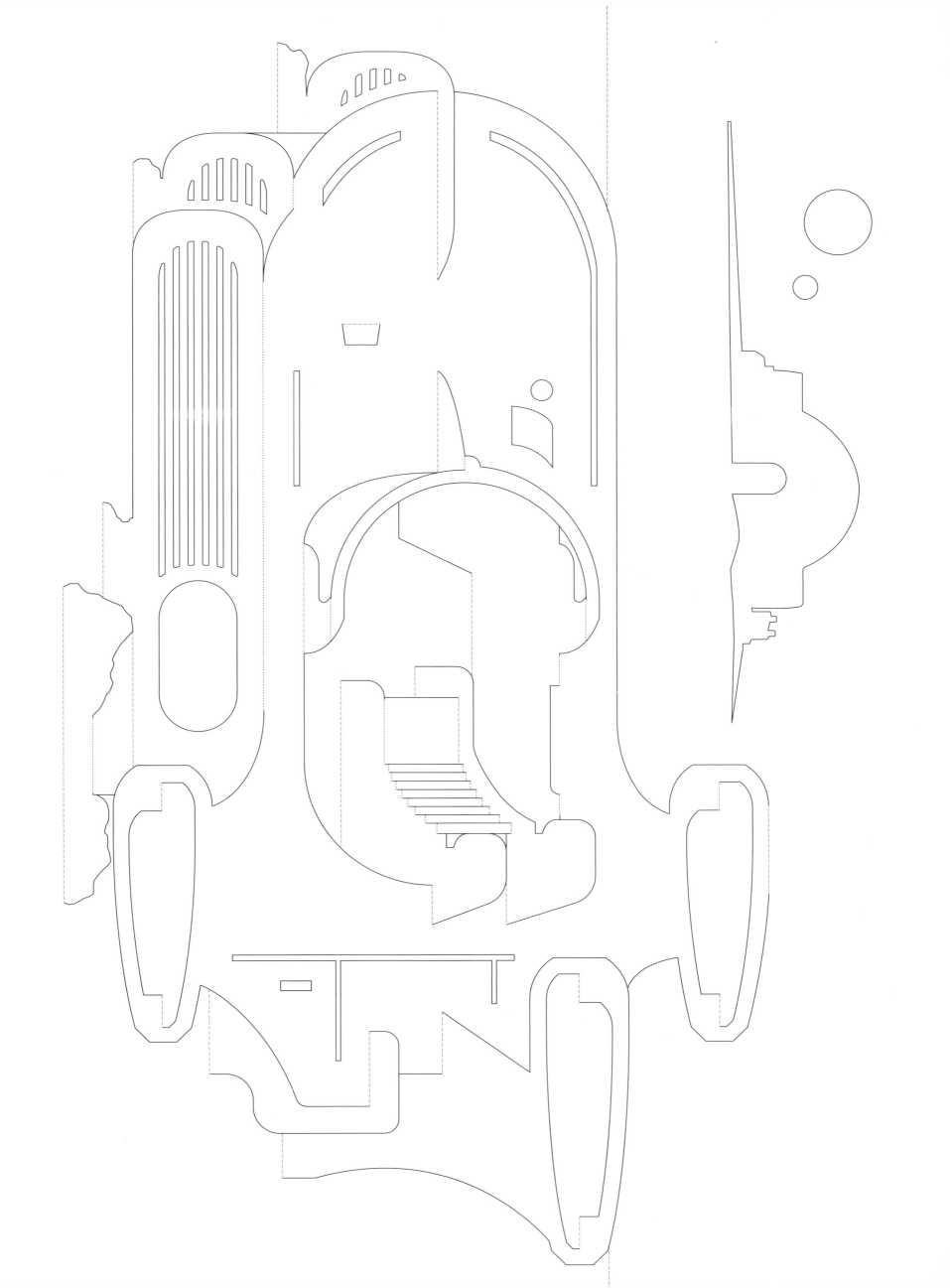

THE SANDCRAWLER, CONCEPT ART BY RALPH MCQUARRIE, 1975.

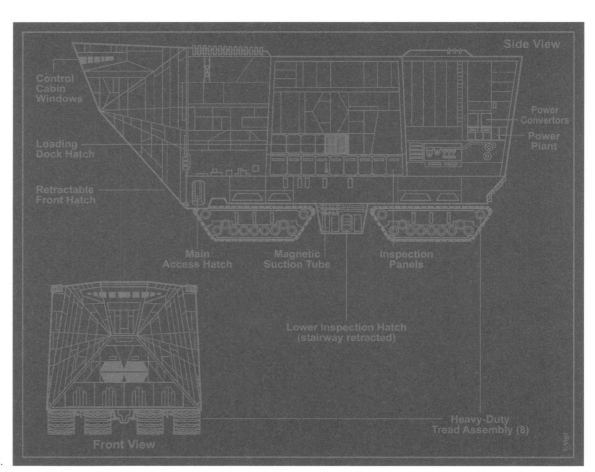

SCHEMATIC OF THE SANDCRAWLER.

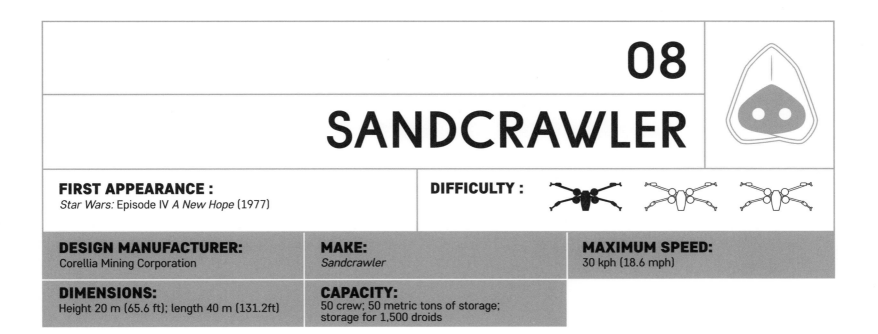

08
SANDCRAWLER

FIRST APPEARANCE :
Star Wars: Episode IV *A New Hope* (1977)

DIFFICULTY :

DESIGN MANUFACTURER:	MAKE:	MAXIMUM SPEED:
Corellia Mining Corporation	*Sandcrawler*	30 kph (18.6 mph)

DIMENSIONS:	CAPACITY:	
Height 20 m (65.6 ft); length 40 m (131.2ft)	50 crew; 50 metric tons of storage; storage for 1,500 droids	

AS A KID MORE OFTEN THAN NOT, VARIOUS SHIPS, VEHICLES, AND BUILDINGS SPARKED AN INQUISITIVE APPETITE IN ME FAR BEYOND THE MAIN STORY AND CHARACTERS OF *STAR WARS.* IN FACT, THAT STILL HAPPENS NOW.

I find joy in focusing on specifics that no one else gives much thought to. One such vehicle that had a particular effect on me was Jawa's sandcrawler from *A New Hope*. I distinctly remember having a insatiable desire to know what was inside it. Even as an adult I'm teased by my imagination. I yearn to know what's behind that door and where that corridor goes. The sandcrawler was no exception. Those small glowing lights from the windows accessed by its huge open ramp had me exploring without seeing. Part of the joy of the *Star Wars* universe is that somewhere down the line, your desire for more information will be indulged. With the sandcrawler, that hunger was eventually satisfied via a somewhat unusual medium. For my twelfth birthday I was gifted some money. I was standing in *Toy Masters* with my mom and brother deciding what to buy; most likely a LEGO set. I have a very distinct memory of my older brother giving me a hard sell and persuading me to buy *Super Star Wars* for the Super Nintendo instead. I'm sure it was an entirely selfless act on his behalf! In retrospect I probably didn't take much convincing.

To my delight, the fourth level of *Super Star Wars* was set inside the sandcrawler. I wasn't disappointed. Rivers of lava and conveyor belts with robotic arms proved a hazardous journey. I used to play the game just so I could explore the levels. I'd map out the

screens but not because it made gameplay any easier. It was all just for fun.

First seen climbing over a dune of the Jundland Wastes, the sandcrawler is our first example of alien life on another planet. The huge tank-like vehicle is a building on wheels. The original concept came from the mastermind of Ralph McQuarrie, and the technical schematics were drawn by Les Dilley and Ted Ambrose. For wide shots, a detailed miniature model was skillfully crafted by artists such as Lorne Peterson and operated using remote control. For the scene where Luke first purchases C-3PO and R2-D2, and later for the massacre site, the lower portion of the sandcrawler was built life-size. Later in preproduction ILM would provide a glass matte painting to recreate the vehicle's upper half.

Although Jawas are renowned mechanics, they did not build their roving homes. Sandcrawlers were in fact manufactured by the Corellia Mining Corporation and, after a failed attempt to harvest valuable resources from Tatooine, were abandoned in the desert by their previous owners. From their traveling workshop, Jawas rove the desert planes scouring for stray droids and shipwrecks. They put to use their natural abilities for repairing and repurposing scrap parts that work just long enough for them to strike a deal and move on.

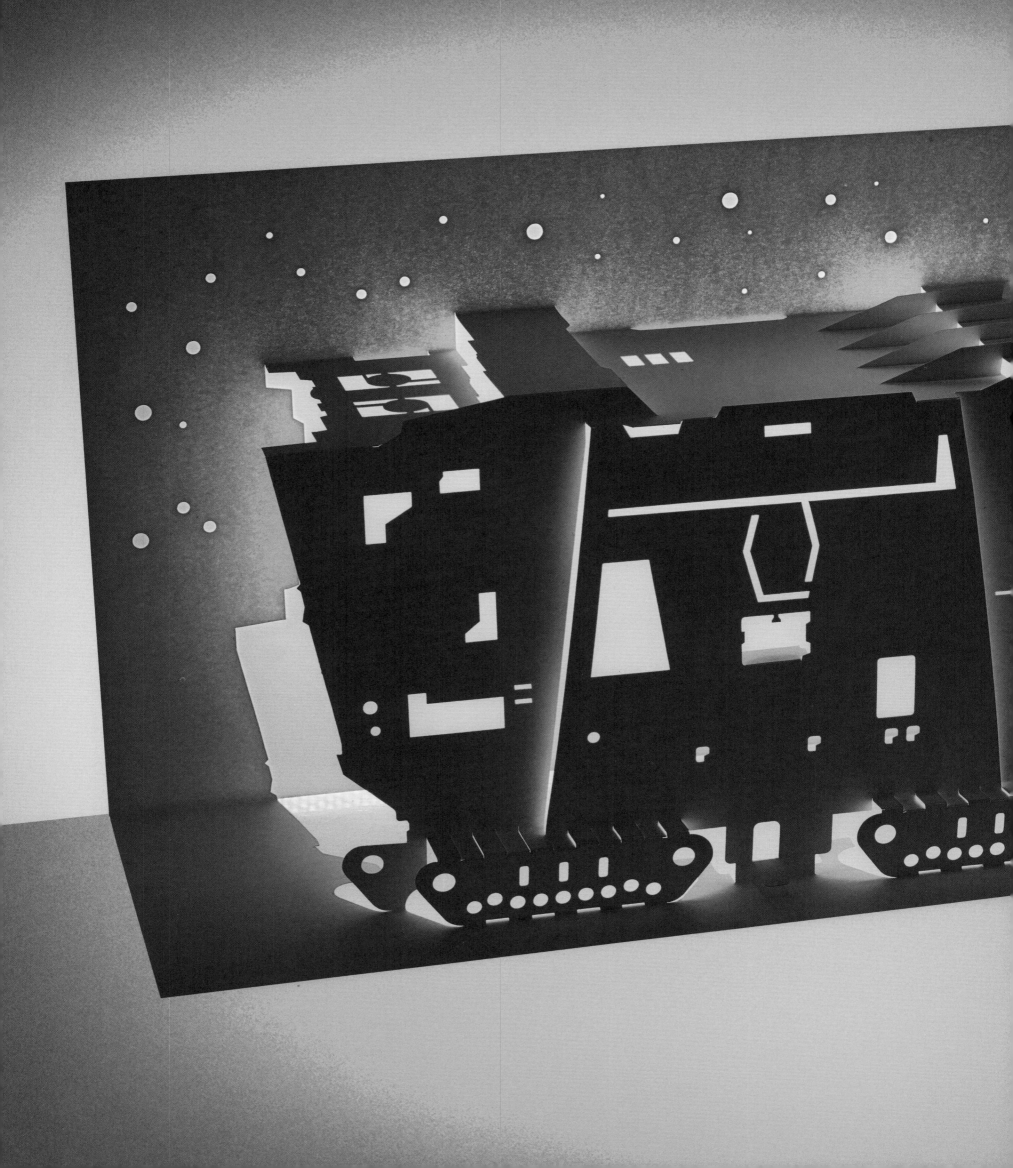

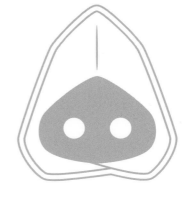

08
—
SANDCRAWLER

CUTTING TIPS

Cut and score the template as per the guide section at the beginning of the book. Cut the inner details such as the panelling, then cut out the stars, as many as you like. Alternatively you could cut out two circles as the twin suns of Tatooine.

FOLDING TIPS

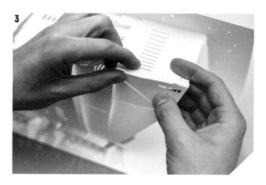

1 With the printed side facing you *lever fold* the main *horizon* line and then *push out* the *valley folds* that form the treads.

2 Rotate the paper 180° and *push out* the *valley folds* that connect the top of the crawler to the *background plate*.

3 Flip the paper over to the non-printed side and *pinch* along the *mountain folds* on the top edge of the crawler.

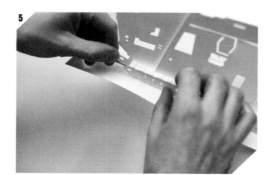

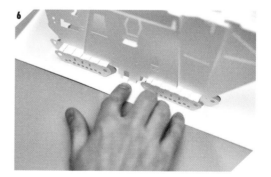

4 There are some small *valley folds* that connect the varying levels of the top of the sandcrawler. Just use the tip of your finger to move these to an upright position.

5 Flatten the lower section of the model—the treads of the crawler should fold fairly easily, though using a *skewer* will help guide the paper as you do this.

6 Be careful that the small area where the doorway is located doesn't crease incorrectly. Once you've flattened the model and repositioned it, you can fold down the small ramp.

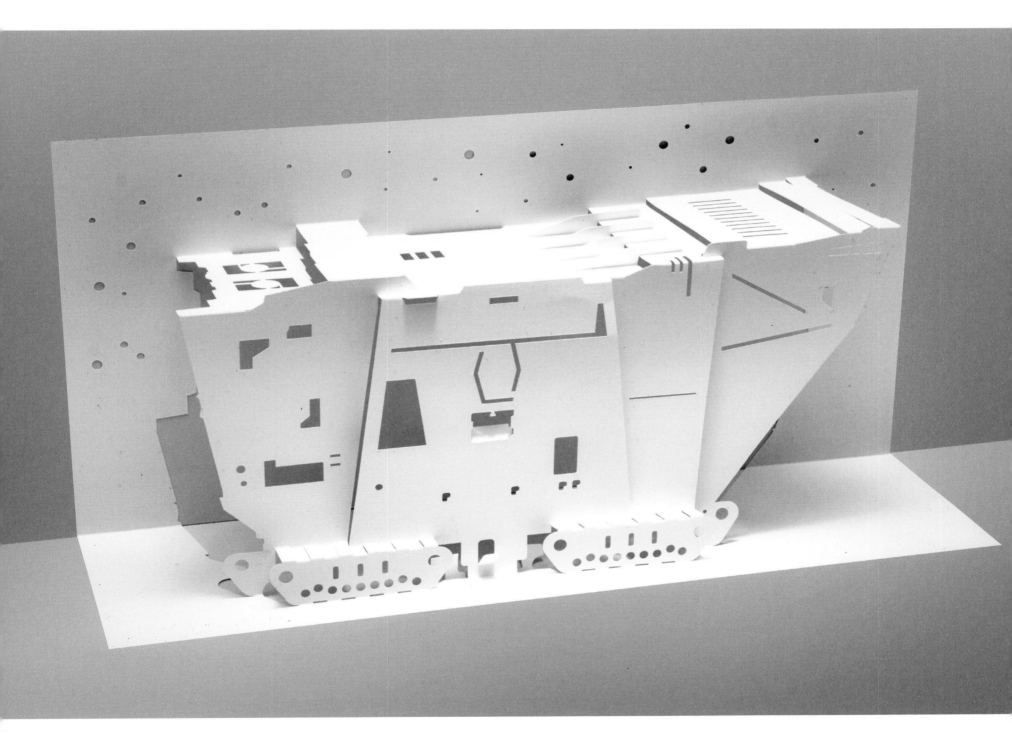

BATTLE OF HOTH, CONCEPT ART BY RALPH MCQUARRIE, 1979.

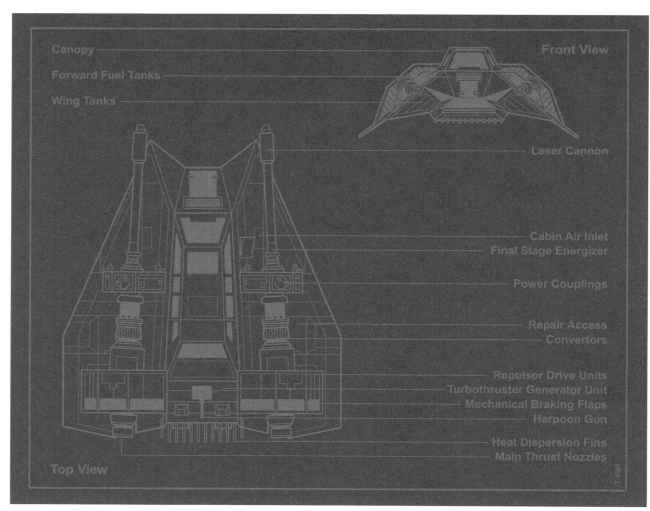

Canopy
Forward Fuel Tanks
Wing Tanks

Front View

Laser Cannon

Cabin Air Inlet
Final Stage Energizer

Power Couplings

Repair Access
Convertors

Repulsor Drive Units
Turbothruster Generator Unit
Mechanical Braking Flaps
Harpoon Gun

Heat Dispersion Fins
Main Thrust Nozzles

Top View

SCHEMATIC OF THE T-47
SNOWSPEEDER.

09

T-47 SNOWSPEEDER

FIRST APPEARANCE :
Star Wars: Episode V *The Empire Strikes Back* (1980)

DIFFICULTY :

DESIGN MANUFACTURER:	MAKE:	MAXIMUM SPEED:
Incom Corporation	Incom T-47 airspeeder (modified)	1,100 kph (683.5 mph)

| LENGTH: 5.3 m (17.4 ft) | CAPACITY: 1 pilot; 1 gunner | |

MANY DIE-HARD FANS SINGLE OUT *THE EMPIRE STRIKES BACK* AS THEIR FAVORITE *STAR WARS* FILM, PRAISED FOR ITS DARKER TONE.

Due to the financial success of its predecessor and renewed faith from the studios, Lucas was able to increase production values for the sequel. This gives *Star Wars* and the intergalactic war an expanded sense of depth and scale. From Dagobah to Cloud City, Episode V is jam-packed with iconic sequences; the war on Hoth is no exception. In an epic David-and-Goliath battle, small yet nimble snowspeeders outsmart their mighty four-legged opponents. Through a stroke of genius from Luke Skywalker, the rebels make use of the backward-facing harpoon gun, tripping up the AT-ATs with heavy-duty tow cables wrapped around their legs. As the biblical legend forewarns, the bigger they are the harder they fall.

The concept for the snowspeeder went through many revisions. Early concepts by Joe Johnston depicted them as armored snowmobiles resting on a trio of skis. After the final design had been agreed, detailed drawings were completed by ILM artist Nilo Rodis-Jamero. Several different, size-scale models were built to serve a variety of special effect methods being used, including motion control and pyrotechnics. The models have motorized break flaps and even the small puppeted pilots would turn their heads inside the cockpit. At one point, an adventurous idea was planned for the smallest of these models to be flown and operated by remote control, therefore negating the need for filming against a blue screen.

Full-size snowspeeders were built as background props for the Echo Base hangar. Another plan, later abandoned, was to place a full-scale snowspeeder on a gimbal so that close-up and interior shots could have a better sense of motion and realism with genuine backdrops. Ultimately, the use of two stagehands rocking the ship from each side was opted for. Perhaps a more "budget-friendly" solution.

Snowspeeders were not initially designed for use in subzero temperatures, nor was the civilian airspeeder intended for such intense battle—evidenced by their lack of defense shields. Once the rebels had established their new base on Hoth, they repurposed a small squadron for use on the frontline. Laser cannons were retrofitted to the wings and rebel mechanics were able to insulate the cooling fins so that the engines wouldn't seize up in the icy climate.

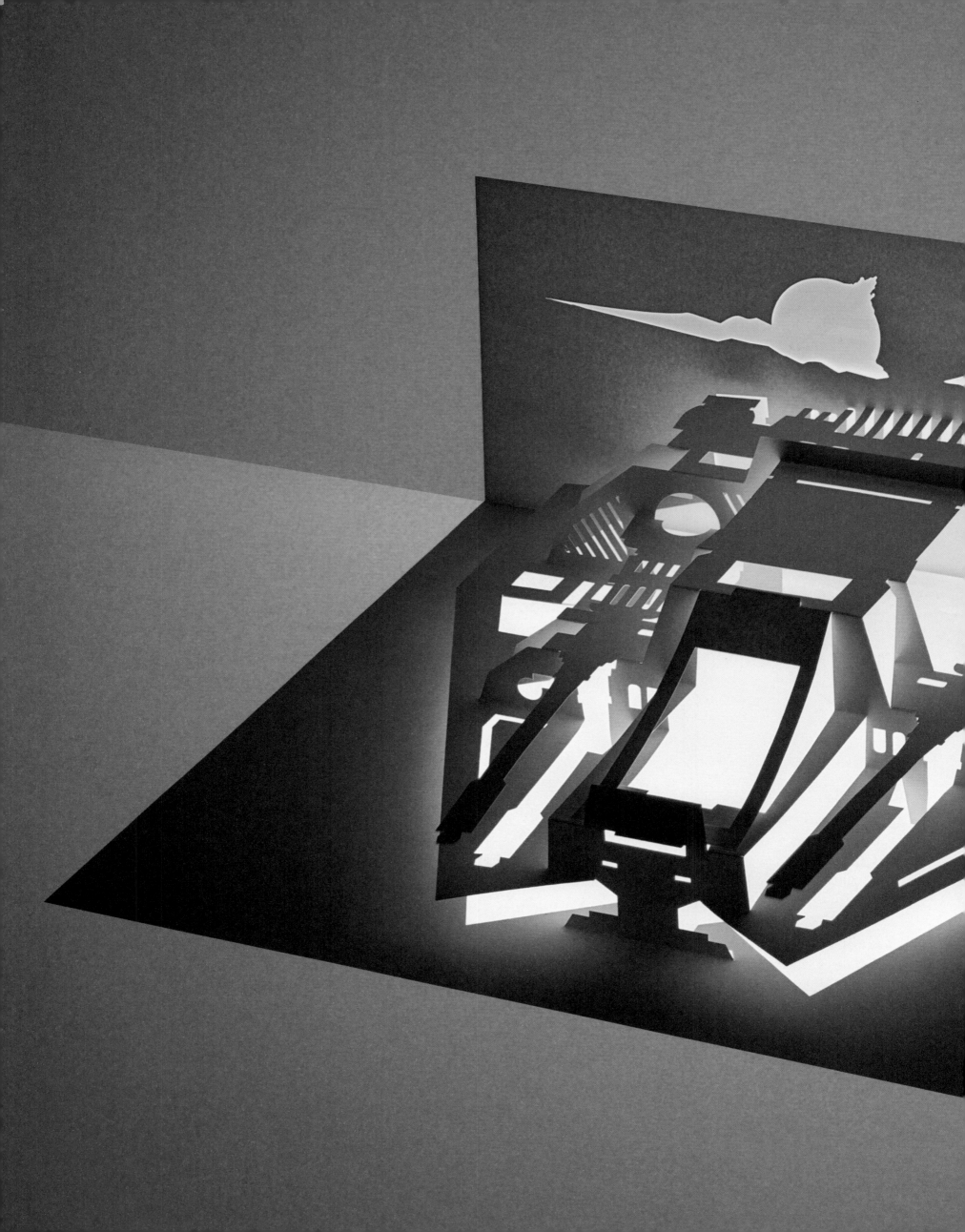

09
—
T-47
SNOWSPEEDER

CUTTING TIPS	

Cut and score the template as per the guide section at the beginning of the book. Cut out the ion-cannon on the background plate first, then cut the inner details such as the panelling and windows.

FOLDING TIPS

1

With the printed side facing you *lever fold* the main *horizon line* and then *push out* the *valley folds* that connect the back end of the speeder and the grill to the *background plate*.

2

Still with the printed side facing you, work your way along the length of the base *pushing out* each of the *valley folds*.

3

Rotate the page 180° and *push out* the landing foot at the front of the ship. Flip the paper over and *pinch* the canopy *mountain fold*.

4

Place the base of the ship on a surface, holding it flat with one hand. Take the cockpit in the other hand and pull the model toward you so that it begins to sit upright.

5

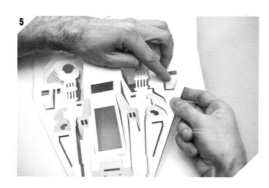

Using mainly the *pinching* method, focus on all of the *mountain folds* on the non-printed side until you can fold it completely flat. Don't forget about the two *mountain folds* that create the support struts, which keep the vehicle raised off the ground.

6

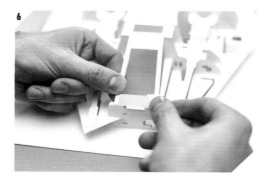

Fold down the cockpit shield to a sloping angle. Place the tab through the slot on the front of the speeder to keep it in a secure position.

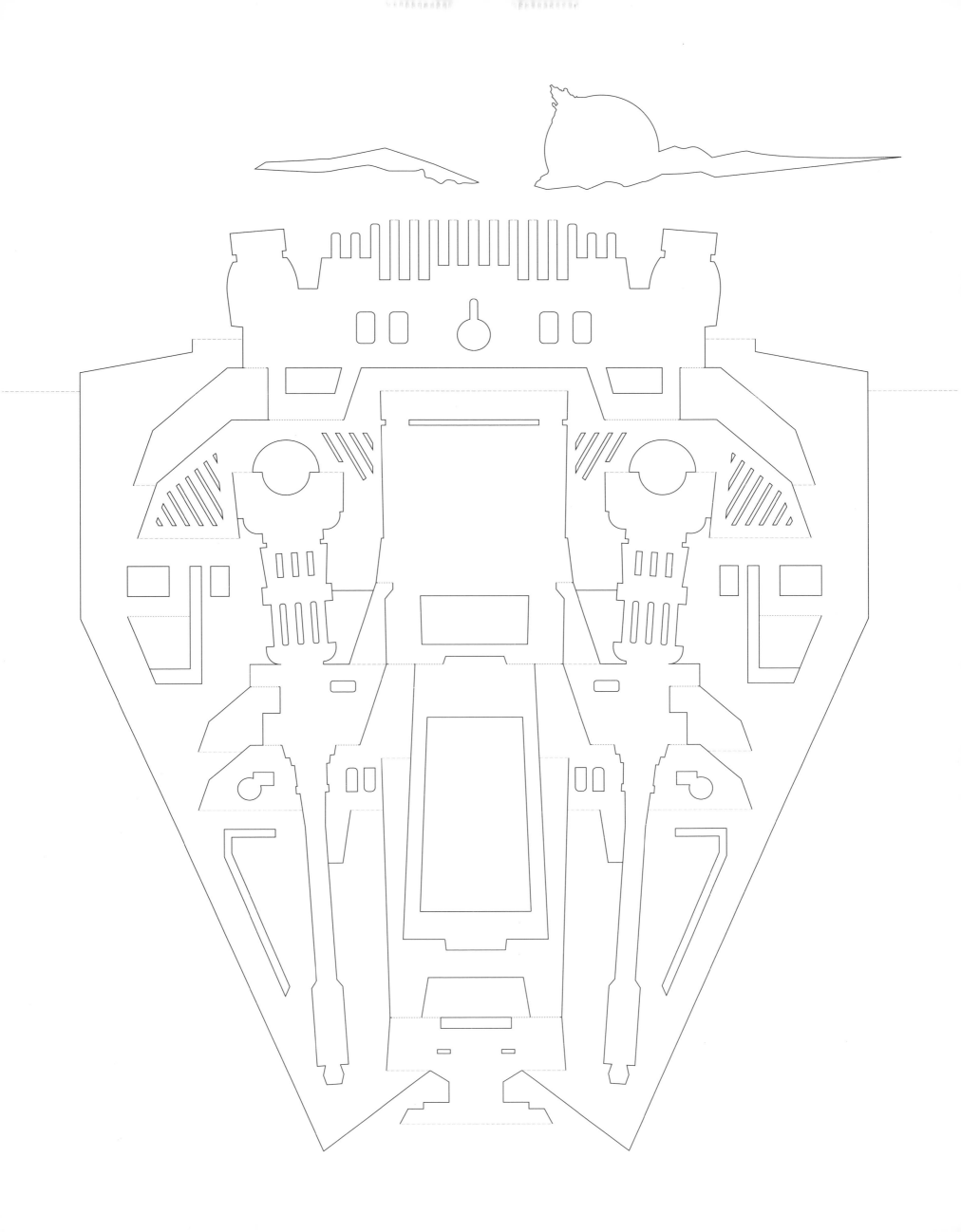

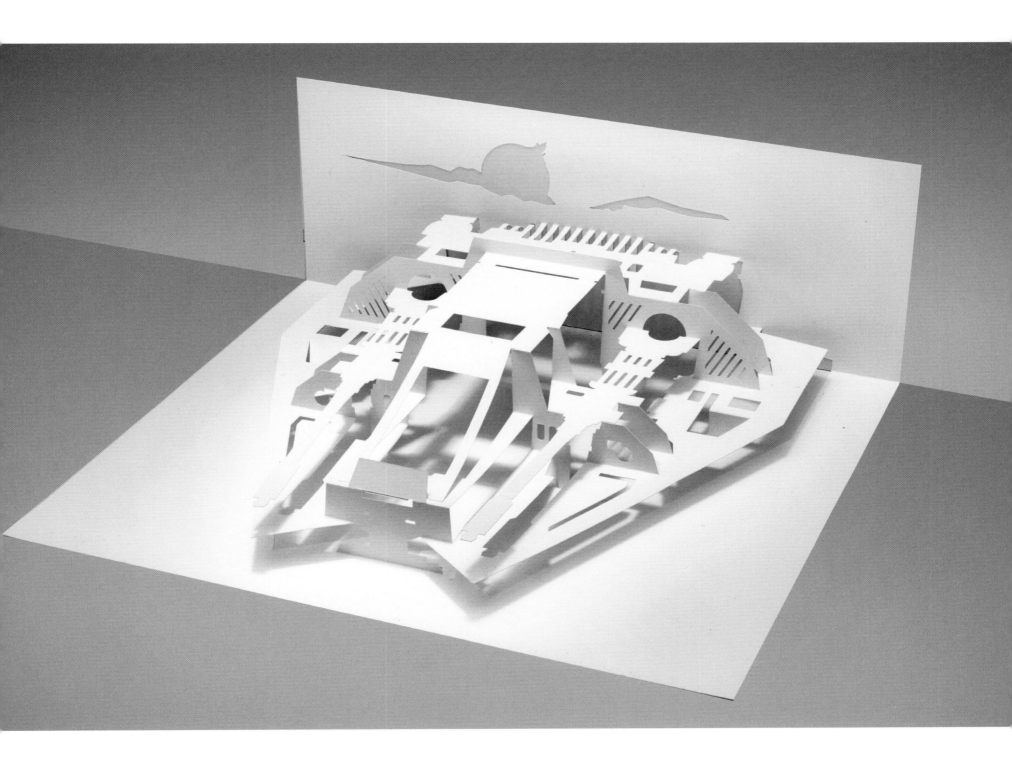

MILLENIUM FALCON AND DOCKING BAY 94, CONCEPT ART BY RALPH MCQUARRIE, 1975.

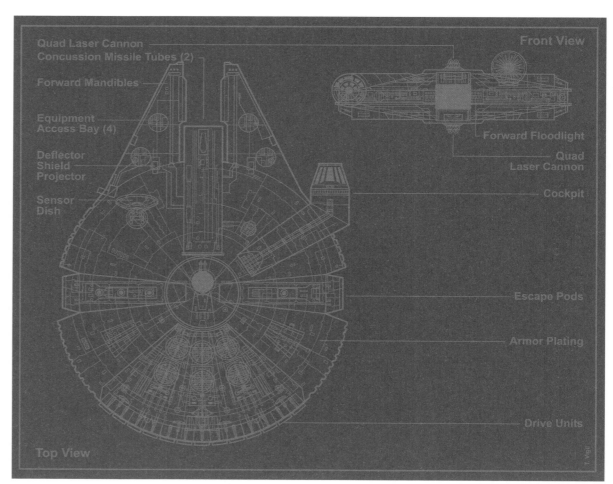

Quad Laser Cannon
Concussion Missile Tubes (2)

Front View

Forward Mandibles

Equipment
Access Bay (4)

Forward Floodlight

Deflector
Shield
Projector

Quad
Laser Cannon

Sensor
Dish

Cockpit

Escape Pods

Armor Plating

Drive Units

Top View

SCHEMATIC OF THE
MILLENNIUM FALCON.

10

MILLENNIUM FALCON

FIRST APPEARANCE :	DIFFICULTY :
Star Wars: Episode IV *A New Hope* (1977)	

DESIGN MANUFACTURER: Corellian Engineering Corporation	MAKE: Corellian YT-1300 transport (modified)	HYPERDRIVE: Class 0.5
LENGTH: 34.75 m (114 ft)	CAPACITY: 2 crew; 6 passengers; 100 metric tons of cargo	

THE *MILLENNIUM FALCON* IS NOT ONLY THE MOST ICONIC SHIP IN THE ENTIRE *STAR WARS* UNIVERSE, IT'S ARGUABLY THE MOST RECOGNIZABLE IN SCIENCE-FICTION HISTORY.

The disc-shaped body and asymmetric offset cockpit seem almost the antithesis of the sharp and elongated angles of the Imperial Star Destroyers. Before receiving its familiar moniker, the ship was simply referred to as the "Pirate Ship." A lengthy and difficult design process was well documented in the form of many sketches and paintings by concept artists such as Ralph McQuarrie and Colin Cantwell. For most of these incarnations, the "Pirate Ship" is revealed to be long and narrow with an engine cluster at the rear while the top end bears the conical cockpit that we're familiar with today. This design was so close to being used that blueprints were drafted, a full-scale model was built, and set construction was to commence imminently. Much to the dismay of everyone involved, Lucas insisted that the design be scrapped, concluding that it was too similar to the *Eagle* spaceship from a popular TV show, *Space 1999*. Fortunately the model that had been built was amended and repurposed as the rebel blockade runner. I think that in hindsight this was a huge benefit to the film. In gaining the new *Falcon* design we also received the *Tantive IV* and despite only having a few moments of screen time, it plays an important role in fixating the audience from the beginning.

Joe Johnson was tasked at the eleventh hour to come up with a design for the new *Falcon*. An urban myth claims that the inspiration for the ship design came from hamburger with an olive skewered to the side, although this is somewhat disputed.

For this kirigami, instead of stars surrounding the ship I've drawn asteroid shapes. Did you know that some of the background asteroids in *The Empire Strikes Back* were actually potatoes?

The YT-1300 Corellian freighter came into Han's possession after winning a game of sabacc against fellow smuggler Lando Calrissian. Despite often being referred to in less than favorable terms, through many modifications Solo turned the *Falcon* into one of the fastest and most revered ships in the galaxy. However, through multiple changes of hands and endless modifications, the ship maintains an almost constant state of repair. But despite its shabby (and deceptive) appearance, it remains a labor of love for Han and Chewbacca.

10
—
MILLENNIUM FALCON

CUTTING TIPS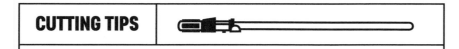

Cut and score the template as per the guide section at the beginning of the book. Start with the panel details on the hull of the ship, followed by the asteroids. Cut as many of the asteroids as you like. Alternatively, you could replace them with a star field.

FOLDING TIPS

1

With the printed side facing you *push out* the *valley folds* that connect the back of the ship to the *background plate*.

2

Flip the paper over to the non-printed side and flatten the *valley folds* of the asteroids that connect the ship to the *base plate*.

3

Still with the non-printed side facing you, fold the *mountain folds* of the ship.

4

Tackle both the *valley* and *mountain folds* of the two mandibles by squeezing their tips together.

5

Fold the *mountain fold* of the cockpit downward.

6

Position the model in its display position and finally tilt the satellite dish to an angle of around 45°.

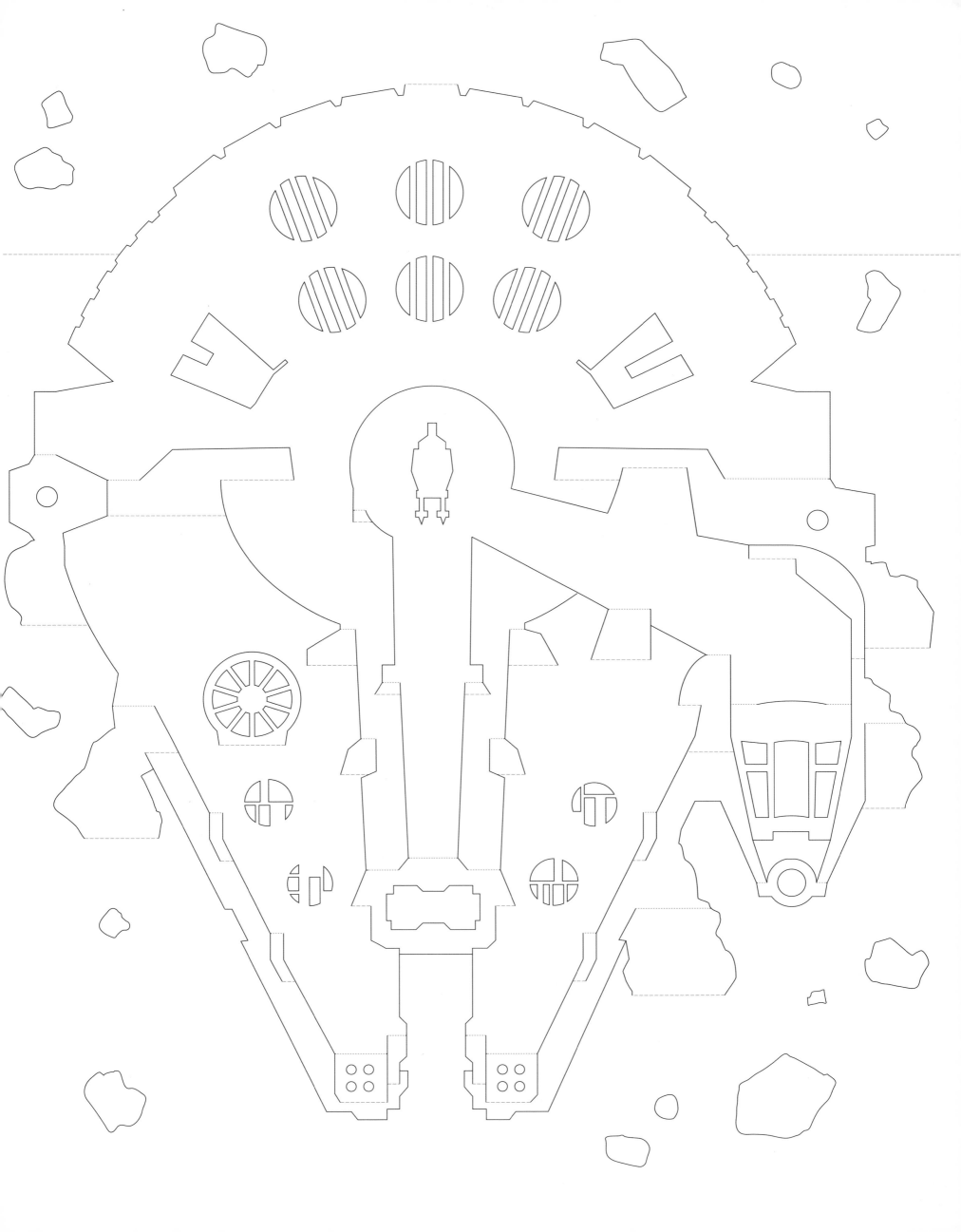

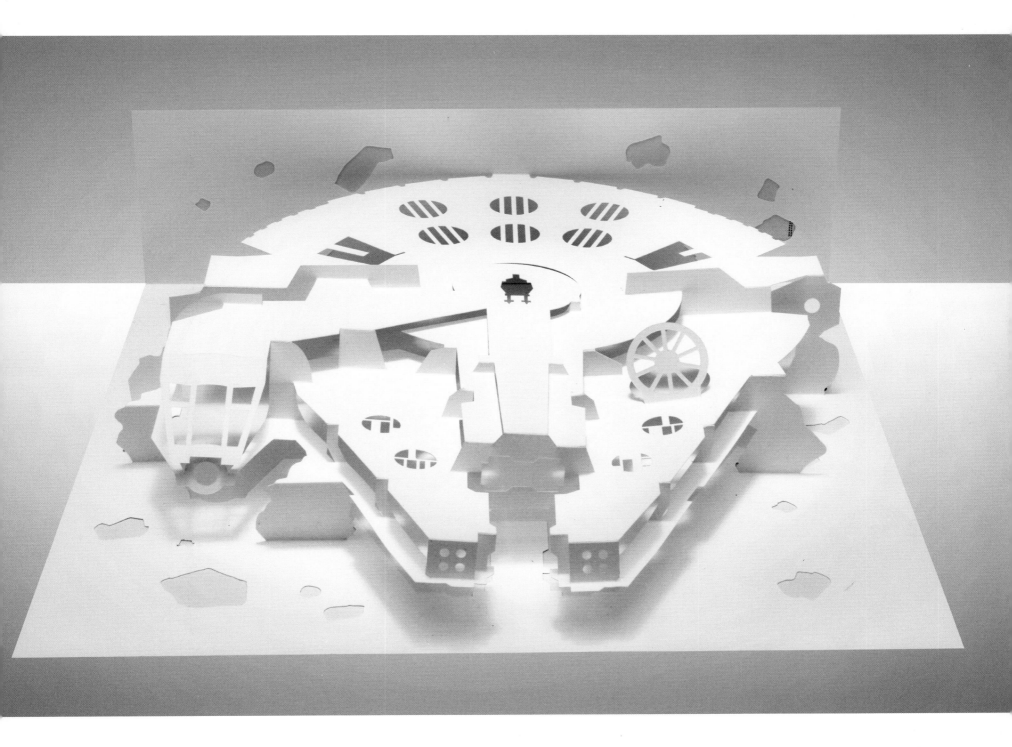

THE MIGHT OF THE EMPIRE LOOMS OVER ENDOR,
STAR WARS: EPISODE VI *RETURN OF THE JEDI* (1983).

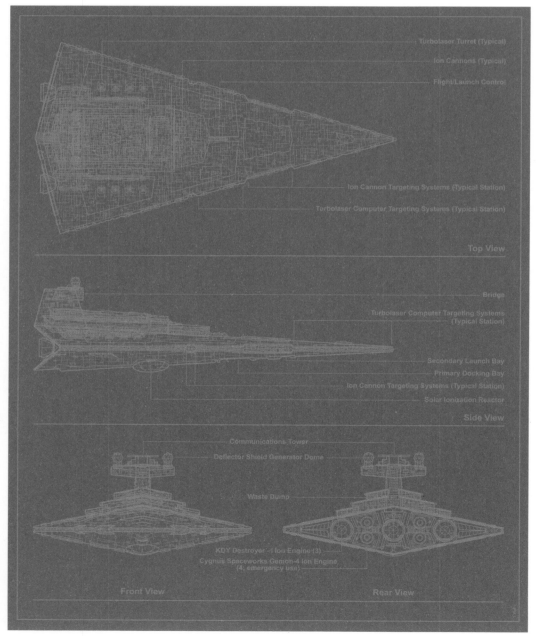

Turbolaser Turret (Typical)

Ion Cannons (Typical)

Flight/Launch Control

Ion Cannon Targeting Systems (Typical Station)

Turbolaser Computer Targeting Systems (Typical Station)

Top View

Bridge

Turbolaser Computer Targeting Systems
(Typical Station)

Secondary Launch Bay

Primary Docking Bay

Ion Cannon Targeting Systems (Typical Station)

Solar Ionization Reactor

Side View

Communications Tower

Deflector Shield Generator Dome

Waste Dump

KDY Destroyer-1 Ion Engine (3)

Cygnus Spaceworks Gemon-4 Ion Engine
(4; emergency use)

Front View

Rear View

SCHEMATIC OF THE IMPERIAL
STAR DESTROYER.

11 | IMPERIAL
STAR DESTROYER

FIRST APPEARANCE :
Star Wars: Episode IV *A New Hope* (1977)

DIFFICULTY :

DESIGN MANUFACTURER: Kuat Drive Yards	**MAKE:** *Imperial I-class* Star Destroyer		**HYPERDRIVE:** CLASS 2
DIMENSION: Length 1,600 m (5,249.3 ft)	**CAPACITY:** 9,235 officers; 27,850 enlisted; 9,700 stormtroopers		

IN 1977, UNBEKNOWNST TO CROWDS SITTING IN DARK CINEMAS ALL OVER THE WORLD, WHAT THEY WERE ABOUT TO SEE WOULD REDEFINE NOT JUST THE SCIENCE-FICTION GENRE, BUT THE FILM INDUSTRY ENTIRELY.

It's undeniable that within the few seconds after the opening crawl, the tone was set—a story of the struggle between good and evil, signified by the appearance of a terrifying Imperial Star Destroyer in hot pursuit of Princess Leia's ship, *Tantive IV.* As it cruises overhead with a rumbling that shook you to the core, the seemingly never-ending command ship implied to us the gargantuan power and the oppressive nature of a malevolent Empire.

Its symmetrical triangular body is organized, ordered and restrained. Like a shark gliding through the ocean of space, its sharp, piercing bow suggests it can penetrate even the strongest rebellion resistance with minimal effort.

Like many of the original concepts, the design for the Star Destroyer came from drawings by Ralph McQuarrie and Colin Cantwell; first appearing as a small triangular ship in the background of a storyboard by McQuarrie. ILM model maker Lorne Peterson told how the workshop progressed this idea into a more aggressive version. I recently visited the *Star Wars Identities* exhibition in London and was lucky enough to see one of the original scaled models used for *The Empire Strikes Back.* I was astounded at how

big the model was and the incredible level of craftsmanship. The process of building the ship involved making the primary structure with plywood and styrene sheets. The next step, commonly known as "kit bashing," involved covering the hull with small cuttings of plastic parts, sourced from other commercial model kits. This gives the impression that the ship is a real functioning machine, and without being able to identify any of these extra components, it gives the illusion of immeasurable scale. These additions came to be known as "greebles" and is still a term used in film model making. At the time, these ancillary parts had no specific function attributed to them; however, over the course of the years, fans and Lucasfilm have retrospectively given purpose to almost every element.

Imperial I-class Star Destroyers are 1,600 (5,249.3 ft) meters long, the sheer sight of which would bully planets into submission. Equipped with an overwhelming amount of artillery, high-ranking government officials, each commanding their own ship, enforced the Emperor's dictatorship by instilling fear; submit to the Empire or feel the might of these warships.

11

—

IMPERIAL
STAR DESTROYER

CUTTING TIPS

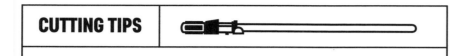

Cut and score the template as per the guide section at the beginning of the book. Start with the panel details on the hull of the ship, followed by the stars, cutting as many of them as you like.

FOLDING TIPS

1

With the printed side facing you, *lever fold* the main *horizon line* and then *push out* the *valley folds* that connect the back of the Star Destroyer to the *background plate*.

2

Still with the printed side facing you, work your way along the length of the base of the ship *pushing out* each of the *valley folds*.

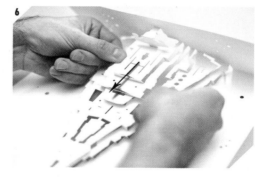

3

Now working from the bridge down to the tip, *push out* all of the *valley folds* of the upper decks.

4

Turn the paper over to the non-printed side. Starting with the bridge, *pinch* all of the *mountain folds* that run the length of the ship.

5

Place the base of the ship on a surface, holding it flat with one hand. In the other hand, take the a section of paper (about ⅔ of the way to the tip) and pull it toward you to help form the structure.

6

Repeat this process with the upper deck. Pay attention to the bridge so that it doesn't buckle and crease in the wrong place. Guide the paper in this direction until you can switch to folding it flat.

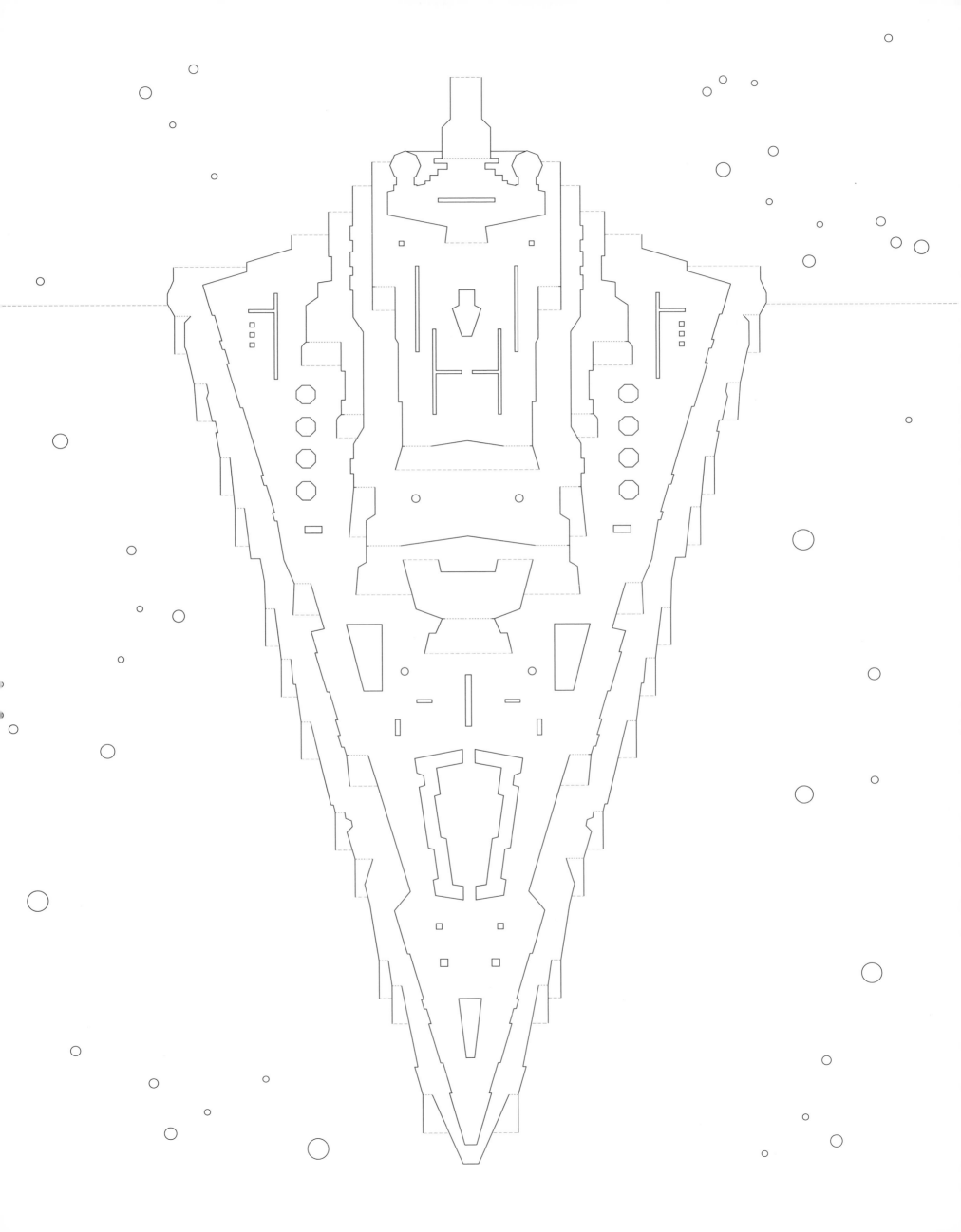

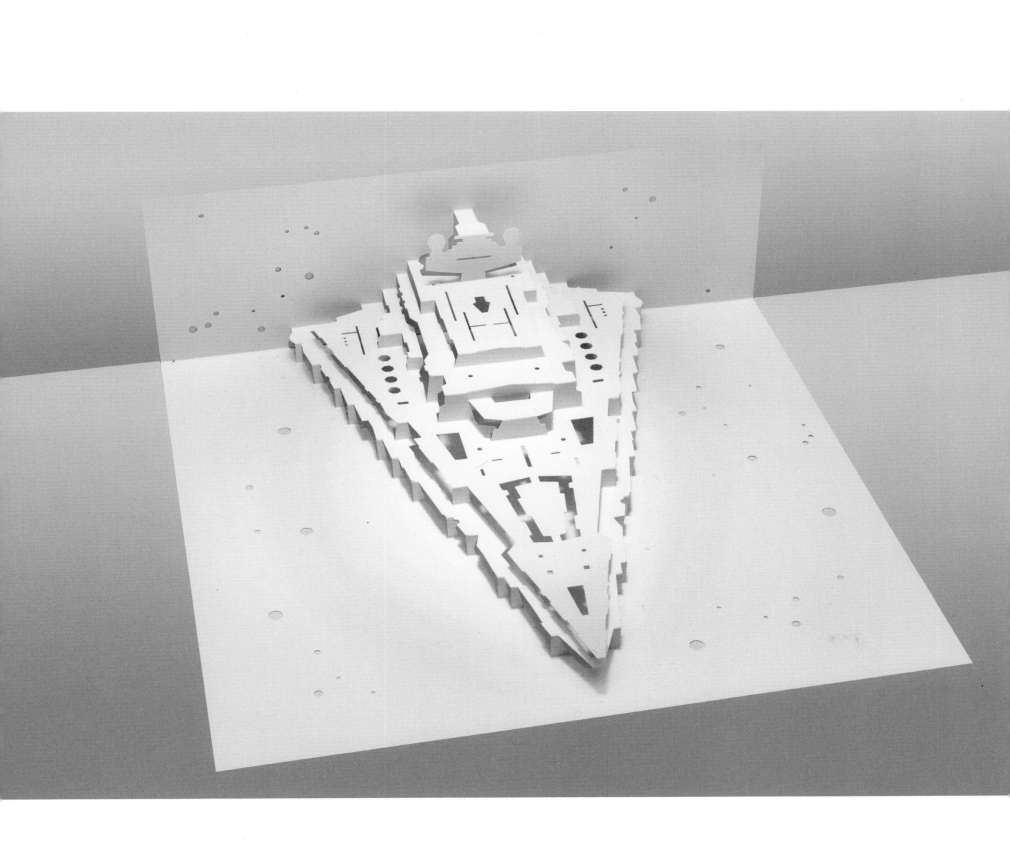

X-WING AND TIE FIGHTER DOGFIGHT, CONCEPT ART BY RALPH MCQUARRIE, 1975.

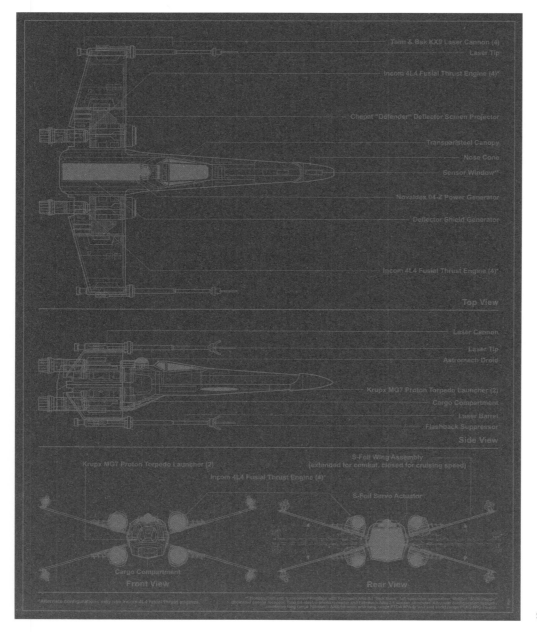

SCHEMATIC OF AN X-WING.

	12	
	X-WING	

FIRST APPEARANCE :
Star Wars: Episode IV *A New Hope* (1977)

DIFFICULTY :

DESIGN MANUFACTURER: Incom Corporation	**MAKE:** Incom T-65	**HYPERDRIVE:** CLASS 1
DIMENSION: Length 13.4 m (41 ft)	**CAPACITY:** 1 pilot; 1 astromech droid	

THE REBEL ALLIANCE X-WING HAS TO BE ONE OF THE MOST RECOGNIZABLE SPACESHIPS IN THE *STAR WARS* GALAXY.

Original artwork was drafted by McQuarrie before being handed over to Colin Cantwell, one of the first concept designers on *The Star Wars,* as it was first known. It's said he took his inspiration for the X-wing from a throwing dart. Its mechanical wings that spread when in attack position (thus creating the X-shape and namesake) are undoubtedly their most discernable feature and were said to have been designed to mimic a cowboy rapidly drawing his guns. The concept in principle remained; however, the ILM model builders evolved the design. One practical reason for this was to create a much bulkier body so that it could house motors to make the S-foils open and close via remote control.

Only one full X-wing was built for filming. If you study the scene at the Yavin base hangar, the rest of the physical ships were actually perspective paintings on boards, cut out in the shape of the starfighter. The rest of the wide shot was a matte painting which would be added later in post-production. A set piece of the cockpit only was made for filming close-ups of the pilots. The eagle-eyed amongst fans will notice

that the S-foils are already in attack position even before the command to do so was given—this was because the set piece was constructed with them permanently open.

The classic X-wing design was resurrected for *The Force Awakens* with several updates. Most notably, instead of four cylindrical engines, the wings now have two, one on either side, that split in half when the S-foils are in attack position. This may have been a completely new design on screen but if you refer back to one of the very first paintings of McQuarrie, you can see the design has been around from the beginning.

X-wing starfighters were manufactured by Incom Corporation. Their mechanical wings are designed to aid a smoother flight when closed and increase their range of fire when open. A single pilot is accompanied by an astromech droid and is equipped with powerful artillery, shields, and hyperdrive. Its svelte structure adds maneuverability, making it a competent if not formidable adversary to Imperial TIE fighters.

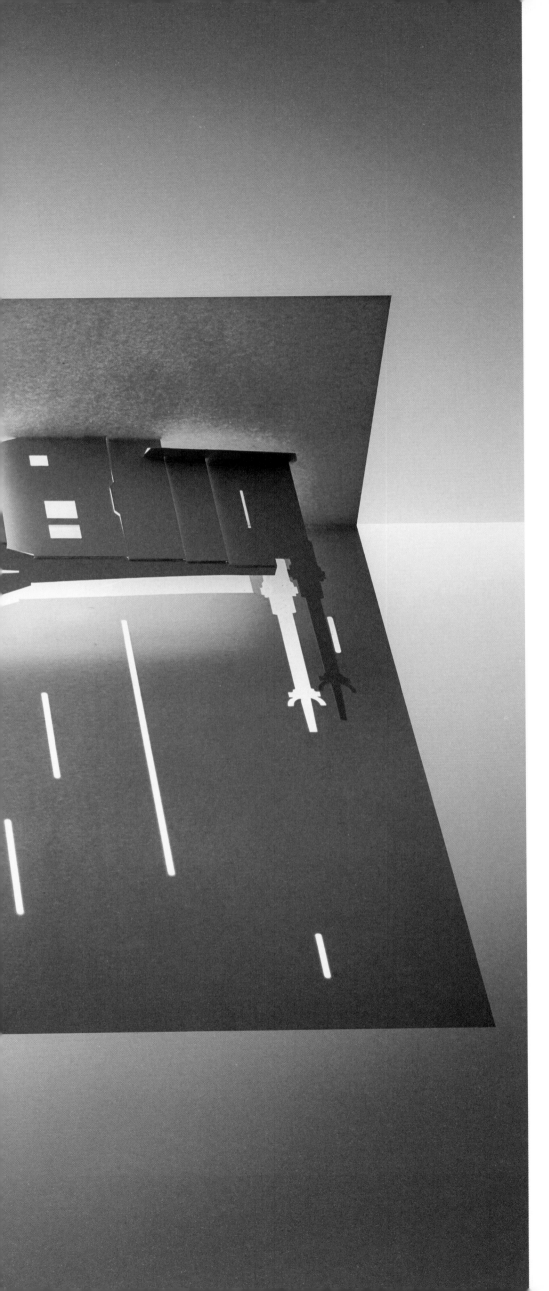

12

—

X-WING

Cut and score the template as per the guide section at the beginning of the book. Start with long streaks of stars, followed by the circular elements in the wing engines.

FOLDING TIPS

With the printed side facing you, *lever fold* the main *horizon line* and then *push out* the *valley folds* that connect the back of the ship to the *background plate*.

Still with the printed side facing you, *push out* the *valley folds* near the nose of the ship and the wing engines.

Turn the paper over to the non-printed side and *pinch* the *mountain folds,* along the wings, the main body, the nose, and finally the two on the lower engines.

Turn the paper over to the printed side again and *push out* the *valley folds* that connect the nose of the ship to the main body.

Place the base of the ship on a surface, holding it flat with one hand. In the other hand, take the main body of the ship and pull it toward you. Guide the paper in this direction until you can switch to folding it flat.

Open the model again into its display position and tilt R2-D2 upright. Finally, crease the cockpit windshield *valley fold* and place the tabs into the slot.

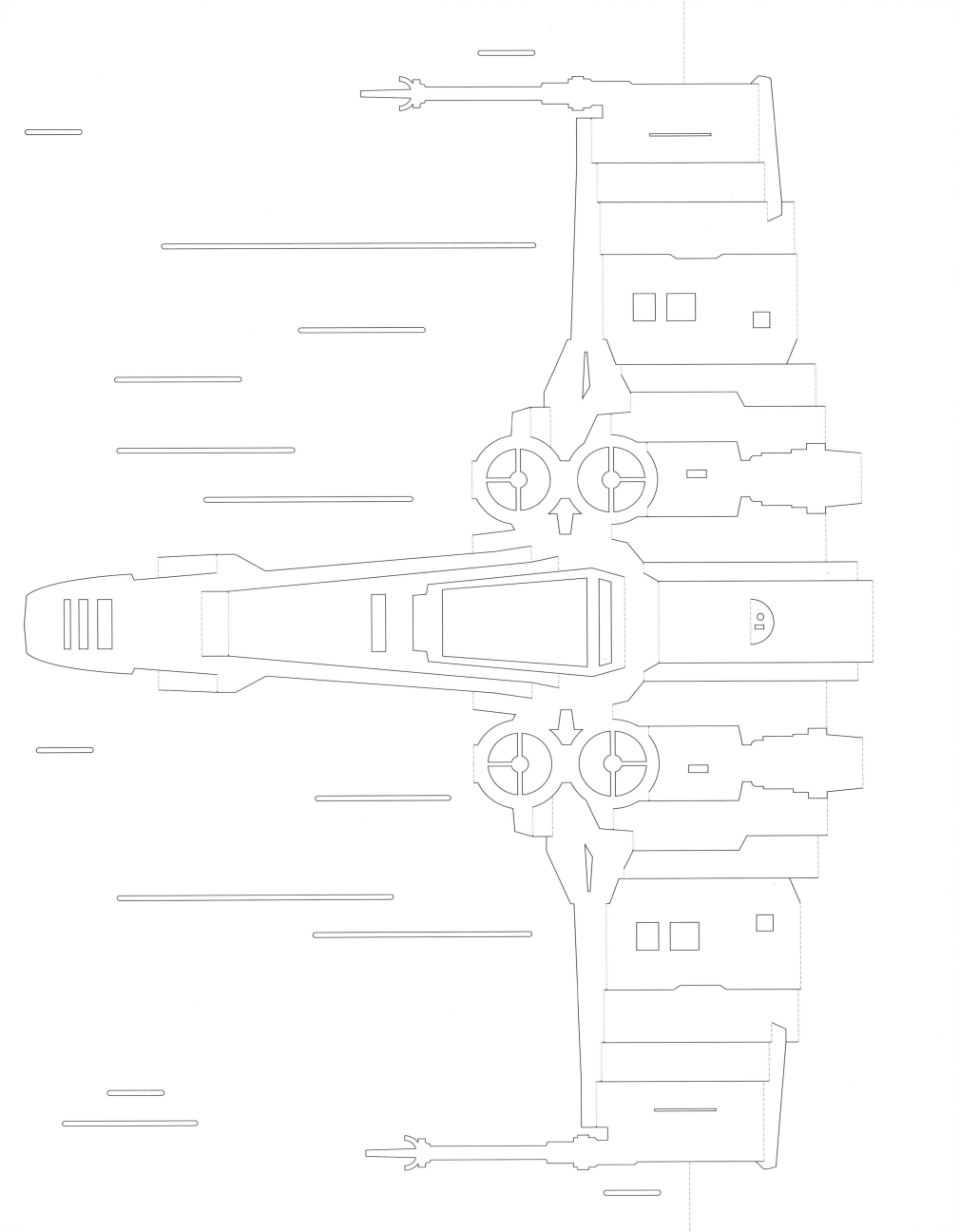

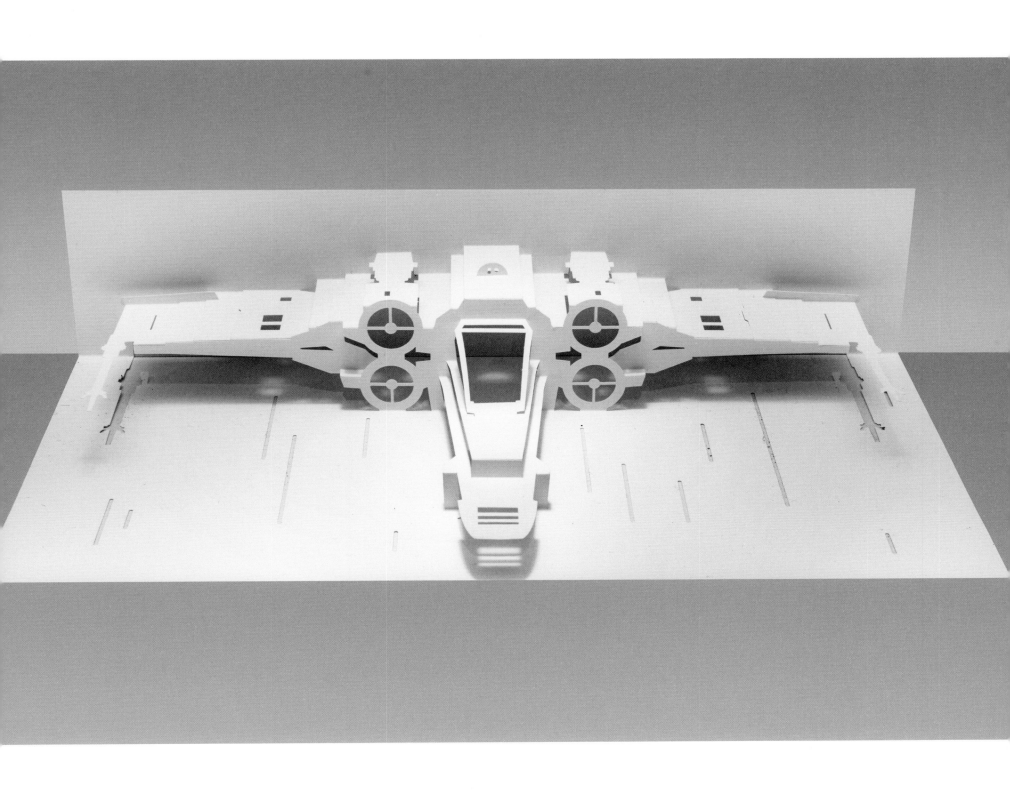

REY ON HER CUSTOM-BUILT SPEEDER, *STAR WARS:* EPISODE VII *THE FORCE AWAKENS* (2015).

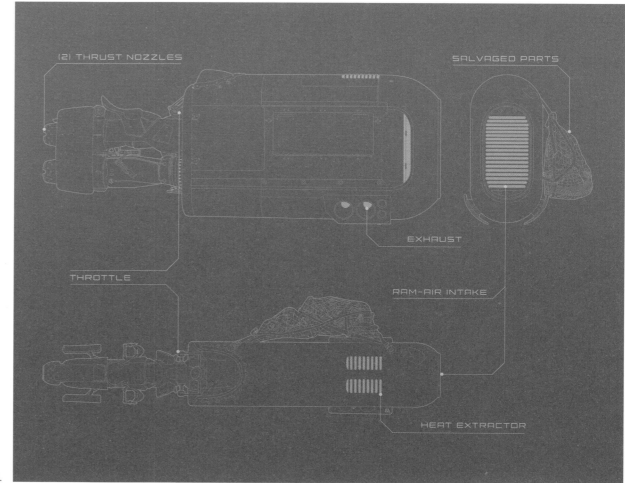

SCHEMATIC OF REY'S SPEEDER.

	13	
	# REY'S SPEEDER	

FIRST APPEARANCE :
Star Wars: Episode VII *The Force Awakens* (2015)

DIFFICULTY :

DESIGN MANUFACTURER: None	**MODEL:** *Customized repulsorlift vehicle*	**MAXIMUM SPEED:** Unknown
LENGTH: 3.73 m (12.24 ft)	**CAPACITY:** 1 pilot	

AFTER AN ALMOST 10-YEAR HIATUS, THE GLIMPSE OF REY'S SPEEDER IN THE FIRST TEASER FOR *THE FORCE AWAKENS* TRANSPORTED US BACK INTO THE *STAR WARS* UNIVERSE AT LIGHTSPEED.

The parallels with Luke's landspeeder were immediately obvious but somehow it was apparent that time had passed and the galaxy had moved on. This familiarity assured us that we were in safe hands with J.J. Abrams's *Star Wars* evolution.

Rey's speeder was no different to most of the key vehicles in *Star Wars* in that it also went through an arduous design process with multiple versions drafted. The earliest concepts of Rey's speeder, or *Kira* as she was initially named, created by artists Dusseault and McCaig, resemble a speeder bike, akin to those used by the Empire on Endor. Another version, assuming at this stage that the artists knew Rey was to be a scavenger, was adapted so that it had the capacity to transport scrap metal. This design by Ryan Church is more in the guise of a sled, brimming with miscellaneous salvage. When several designs are rejected from the art department, it's not uncommon for concept artists from other areas of the production to be invited to pitch ideas. The chosen design was created by Jake Lunt Davies—a creature concept artist who is also credited with designing BB-8. When I spoke to Jake, he told me he drew inspiration from agricultural machinery and 1930s racing cars. Lunt Davies said, "If you look closely you can also see that there's a pinch of turning Luke Skywalker's landspeeder on its side." He then added "There's an ethos of simplicity in *Star Wars* that we constantly strive to achieve—that a design can be recognizable from its silhouette or can be drawn with a few minimal lines." It's for the same reason that *Star Wars* vehicles translate so well into kirigami form. I've added a few boulders and sand mounds in order to raise the model from the ground. The silhouette of a decayed Star Destroyer completes the picture.

Rey built the speeder by herself from parts she's collected over the years. The speeder has seen better days. Patches of rust, dents, and scratches are products of the harsh environment. But despite its superficial flaws, its engine chugs dependably like an old tractor; labored yet loyal. Although Rey's speeder doesn't have the hauling capabilities that other scavengers' might have, it's suggested she favors speed over capacity. A smaller payload is easier to defend. After a long day scouring the Jakku junkfields, she carries her findings in netting fitted to the side of the speeder. She later sells anything of value to Unkar Plutt in exchange for food rations, often meager in size.

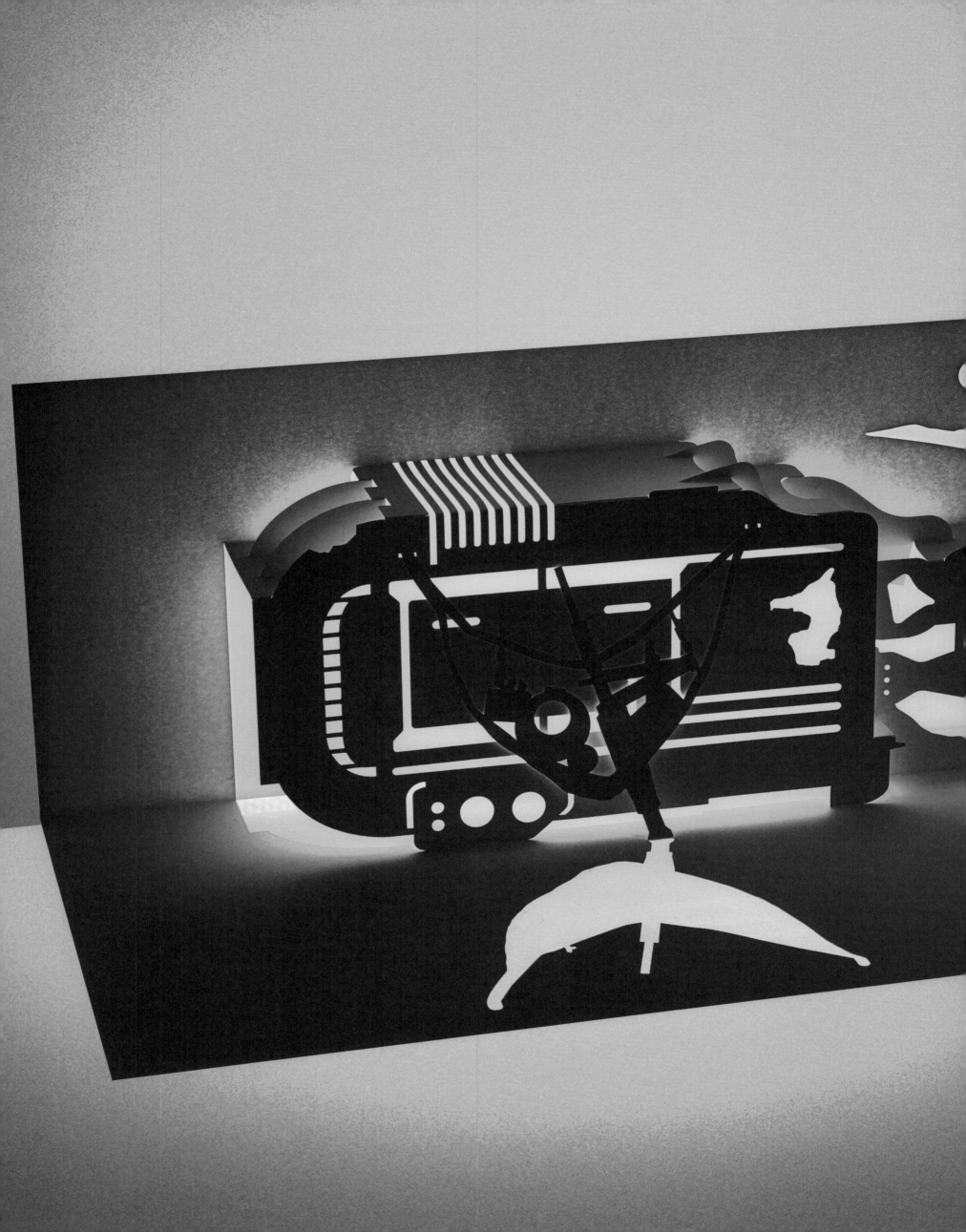

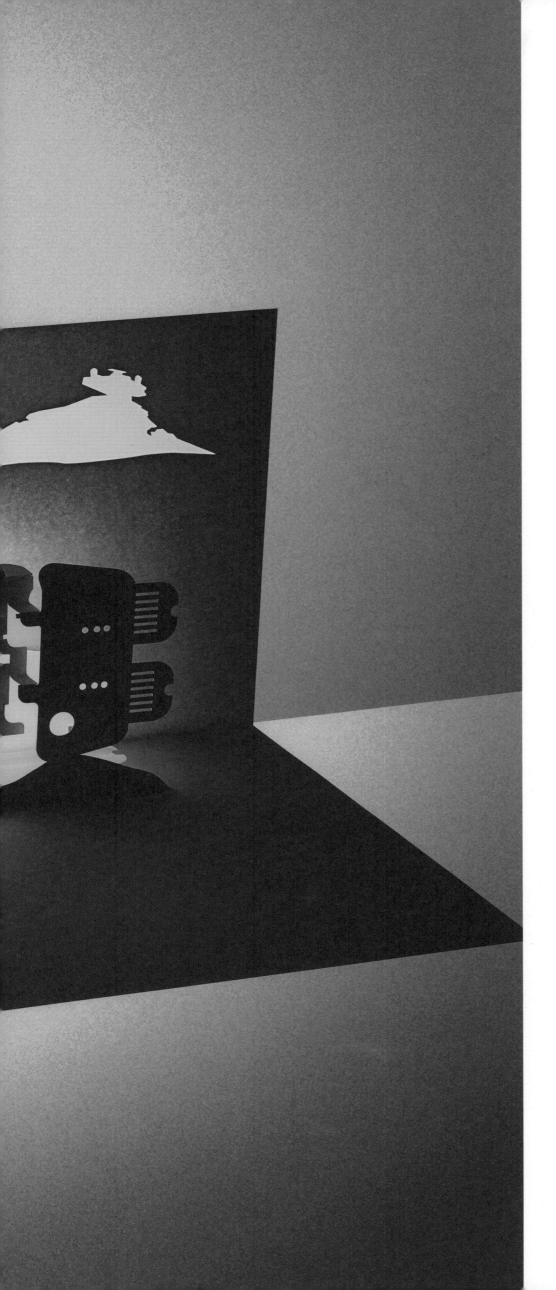

13
—
REY'S SPEEDER

CUTTING TIPS	

Cut and score the template as per the guide section at the beginning of the book. The cargo net is optional; it'll still look great without it, but if you want to include it, start by cutting here. Pay extra care while cutting the grill details on top of the speeder.

FOLDING TIPS

With the printed side facing you, *lever fold* the main *horizon line* and then push out the *valley folds* that connect the base of the speeder to the *base plate*.

Still with the printed side facing you, *push out* the *valley folds* that connect the top of the speeder to the *background plate*.

Turn the paper over to the non-printed side and use a *skewer* to fold the *mountain folds* that run along the top of the speeder.

It should be easy enough to *pinch* the remaining *mountain folds*.

With one hand holding the base of the model on a flat surface, use the other hand to guide folding it flat along the *horizon fold*.

Unfold into the display position and prop up the netting detail. Place the tips of the net into the two small slots on the side of the speeder.

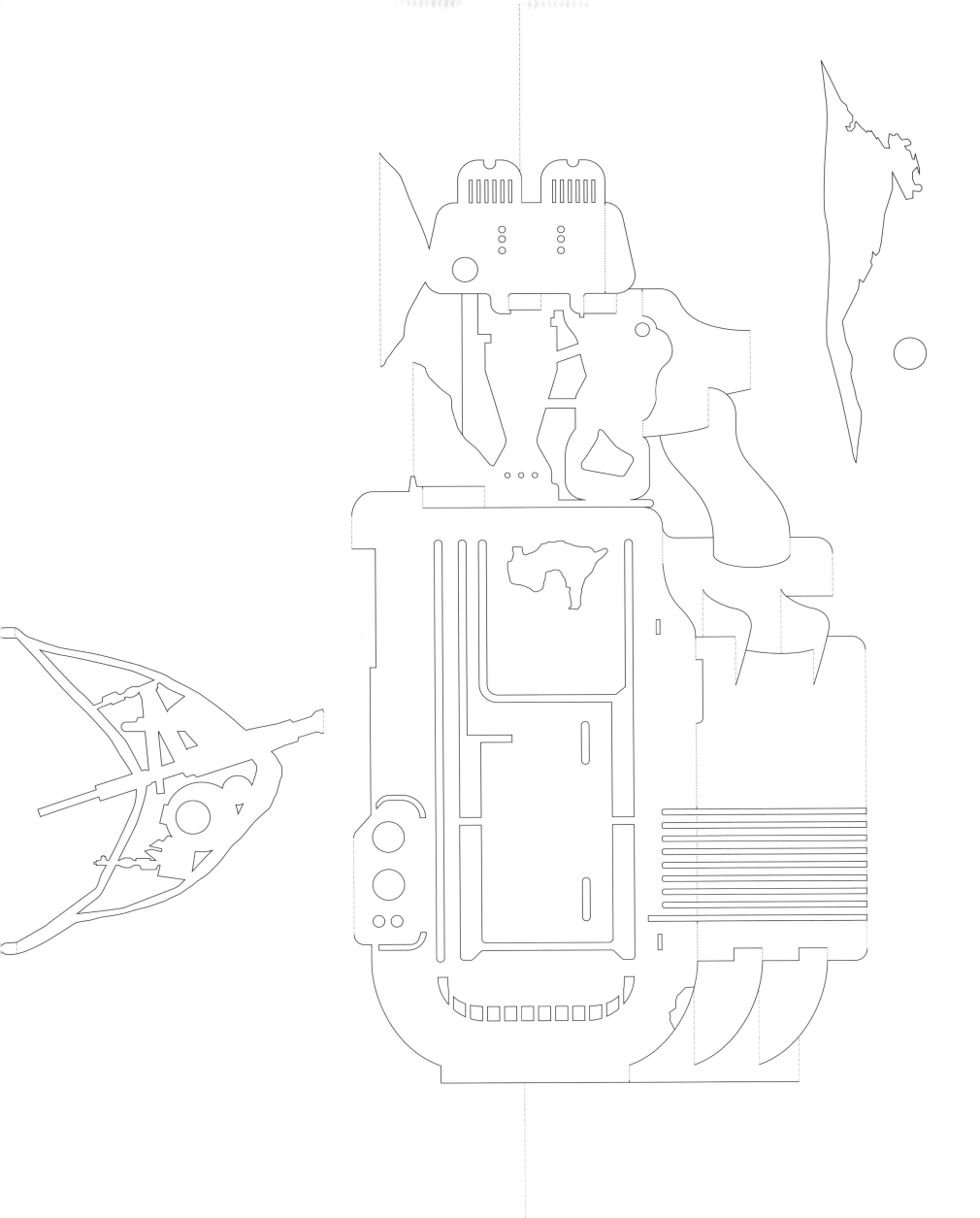

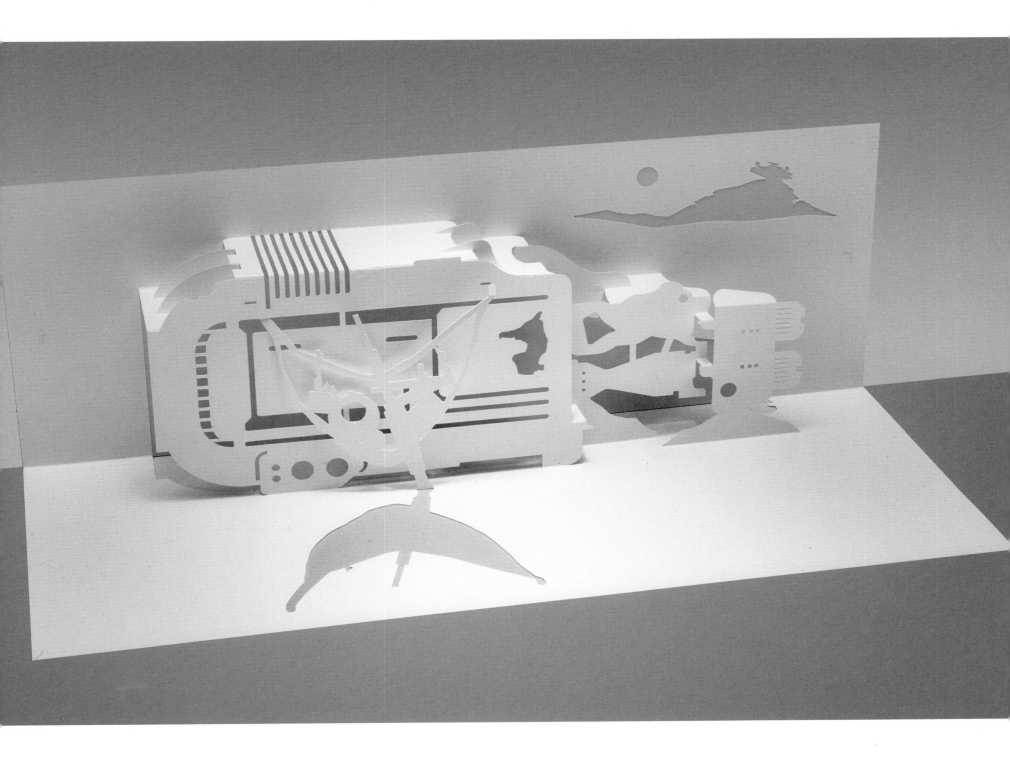

TWO FIRST ORDER SPECIAL FORCES TIE FIGHTERS FROM *STAR WARS:* EPISODE VII *THE FORCE AWAKENS* (2015).

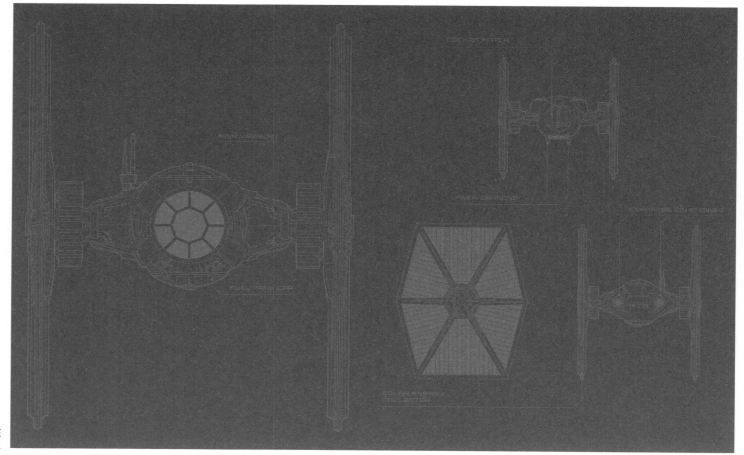

SCHEMATIC OF THE
SF TIE FIGHTER.

	14
# SF TIE FIGHTER	

FIRST APPEARANCE :
Star Wars: Episode VII *The Force Awakens* (2015)

DIFFICULTY :

DESIGN MANUFACTURER: Sienar-Jaemus Fleet Systems	**MAKE:** *TIE/sf space superiority fighter*	**MAXIMUM ACCELERATION:** 2 780G (in open space)
WIDTH: 6.69 m (21.96 ft)	**CAPACITY:** 1 pilot; 1 gunner	

FROM THE UNMISTAKABLE OCTAGONAL COCKPIT WINDOW TO THE HARROWING AND UNFORGETTABLE ENGINE HOWL, LITTLE CHANGED FOR THE NEW FIRST ORDER TIE FIGHTERS—EVIDENCE THAT ITS CLASSIC DESIGN TRANSCENDS TIME.

The beginnings of the TIE fighter and its iconic H-shaped silhouette were born from the pen of George Lucas. Under the heading of "Imperial Fighter," a rough sketch on yellow note paper depicts a long cockpit adorned with two square-paneled wings connected via two delicate spindles. It's dubbed "Finned Sausage." The drawing by concept artist Colin Cantwell that followed kept the elongated body but introduced the more familiar hexagonal wings. At a later stage, the long cockpit was substituted for a spherical one and the overall design bulked out by the ILM model makers so that it would look like a more convincing robust warship.

Initially Darth Vader wasn't meant to have his own TIE fighter design. The decision to create one was necessary so that the audience could identify him amongst the other TIEs. The exterior, like the others, was a miniature model but the interior shots of Darth Vader's TIE Advanced were filmed in the same set piece as the standard TIEs.

There are a few noticeable differences between the original and the First Order TIE fighter. The overall body of the starfighter feels bulkier and is no longer blue. Its darker hull and light gray solar panel wings give it a modernized look. Red panelling signifies the Special Forces unit marking, as well as the addition of a left-hand-side antenna and a heavy weapons turret underneath. One thing remains that confused me as a kid: Why do the bad guys shoot green lasers while the good guys blast red? I'll never know.

With their skilled maneuverability and relentless firepower the original TIE fighters reflected the effectiveness of the Empire. Under the control of the Empire they were instructed to put the goals of the Emperor ahead of their own lives—attacking until victorious or dead. While TIE fighters of the Imperial Navy were seen as dispensable, the modernized First Order SF variant is regarded with much greater esteem. Updated with a limited hyperdrive, basic deflector shields, and improved armament, TIE fighters spearhead the spread of the evil rhetoric of the First Order across the galaxy.

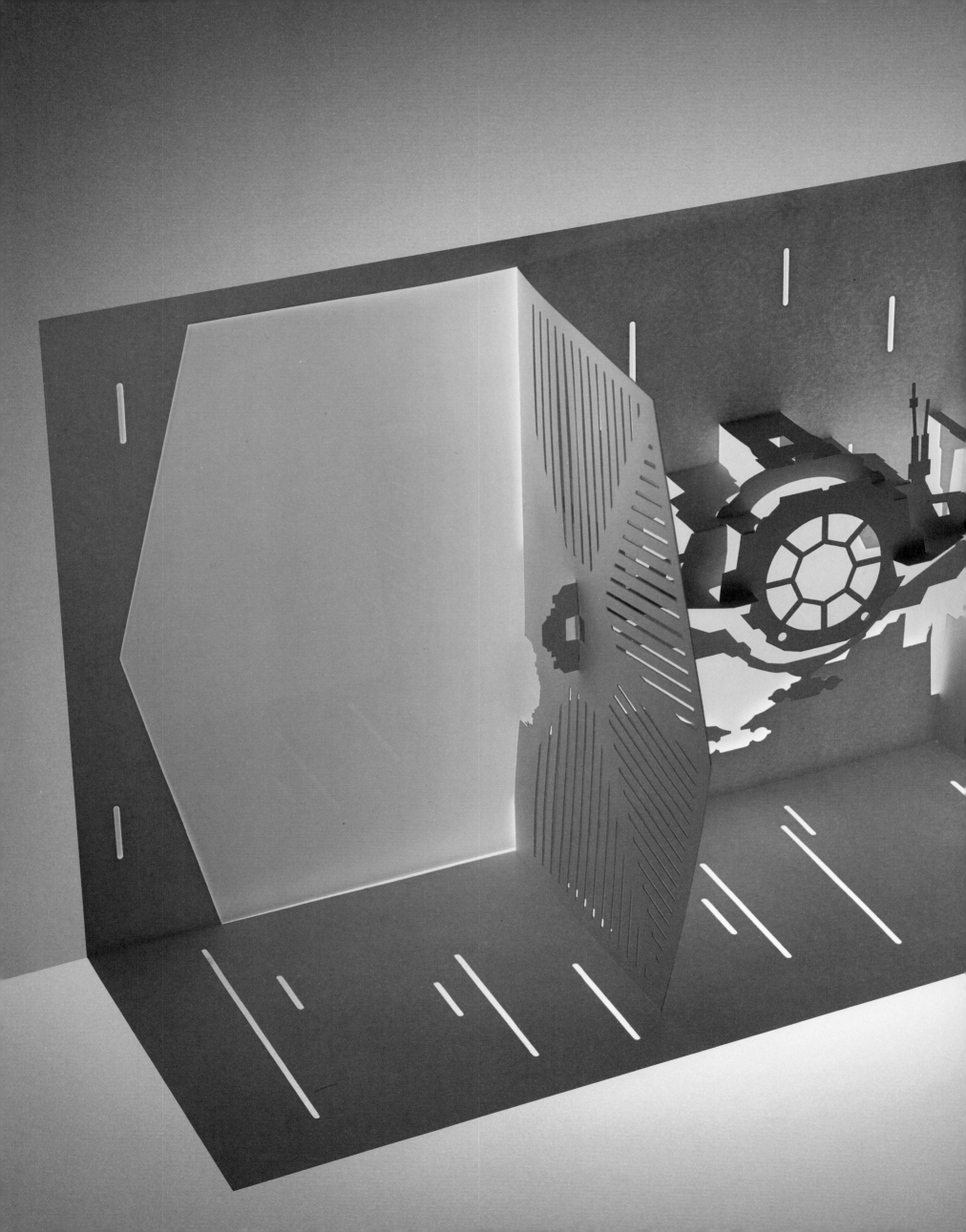

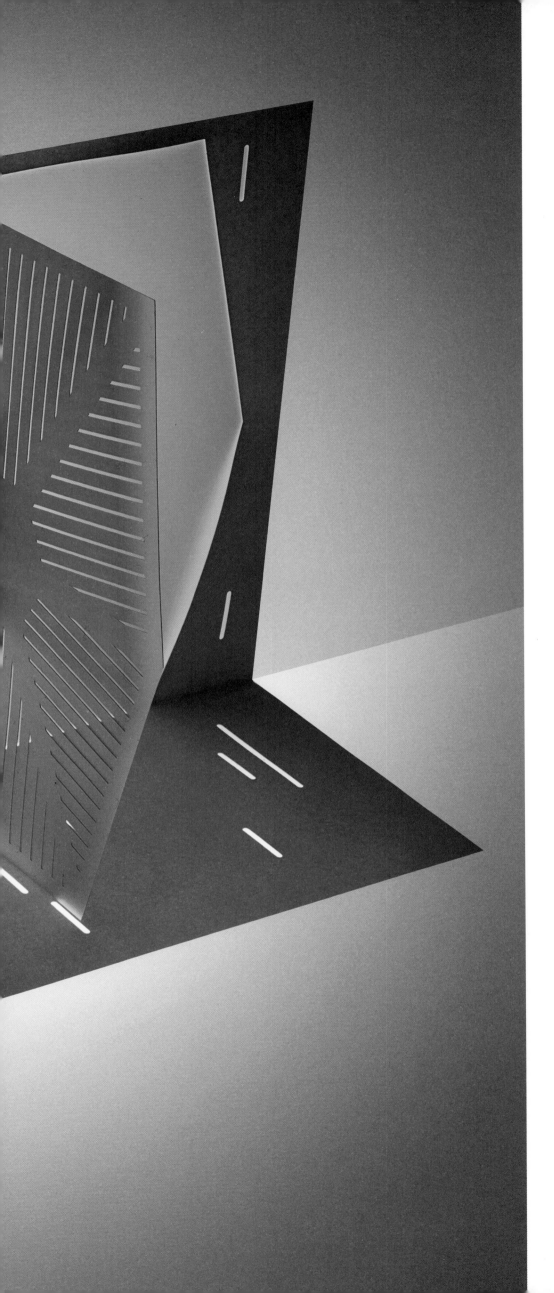

14
—
SF TIE FIGHTER

CUTTING TIPS

Cut and score the template as per the guide section at the beginning of the book. Start with the detailing on the wings, followed by the octagonal window. You might want to leave out the wing details but the result is worth the effort.

FOLDING TIPS

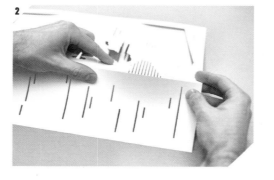

1 With the printed side facing you, *lever fold* the main *horizon line* and fold back to the starting position.

2 With the template set on a flat surface, take one wing and fold it over completely. Unfold it again and repeat with the other wing.

3 With the template positioned upside down and printed side facing you, *push out* the *valley fold* that connects the back of the cockpit to the *background plate*.

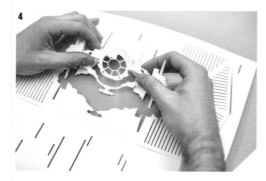

4 *Pinch* the two *valley folds* on the mid-section of the wing struts followed by the remaining *valley folds*.

5 Turn the model over to the non-printed side and *pinch* the *mountain folds*. Taking the cockpit between your finger and thumb, push the model away from you so that you can fold it flat.

6 Again fold in the wings so they are perpendicular to the *background plate* and place the tips of the wing struts into the small slots. You can now sit the model upright.

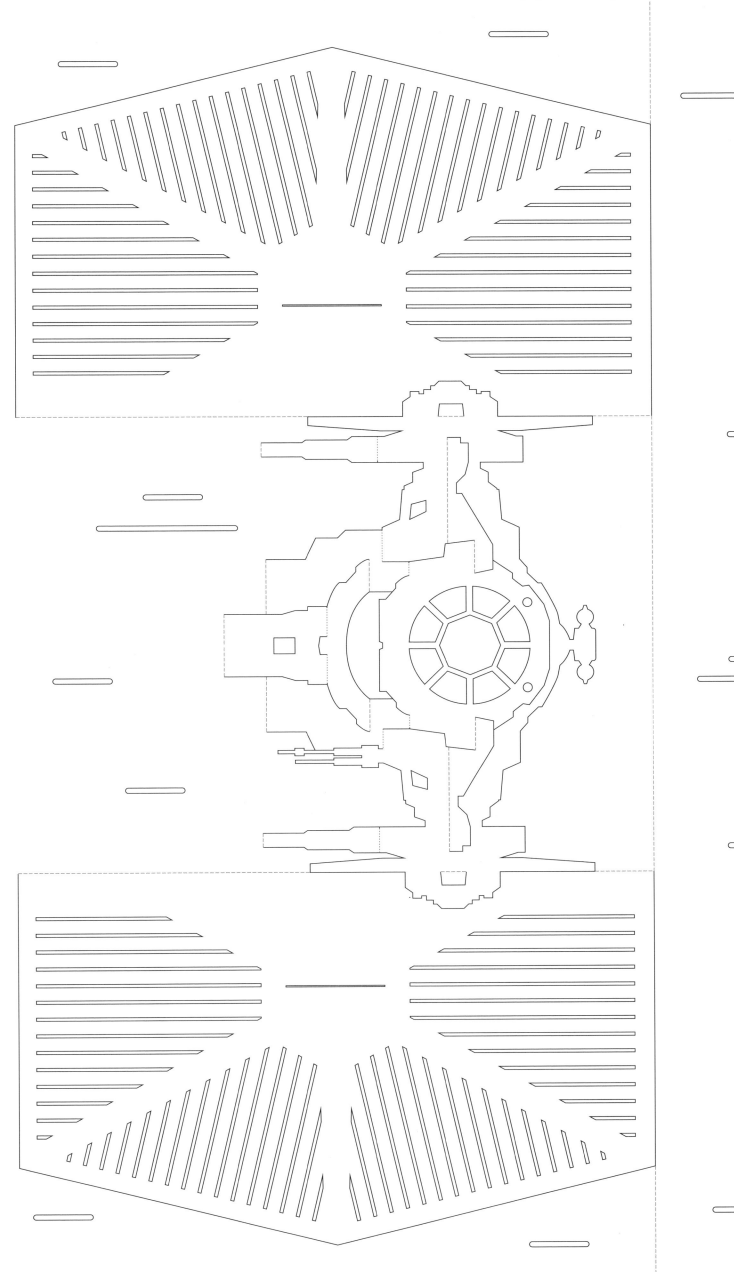

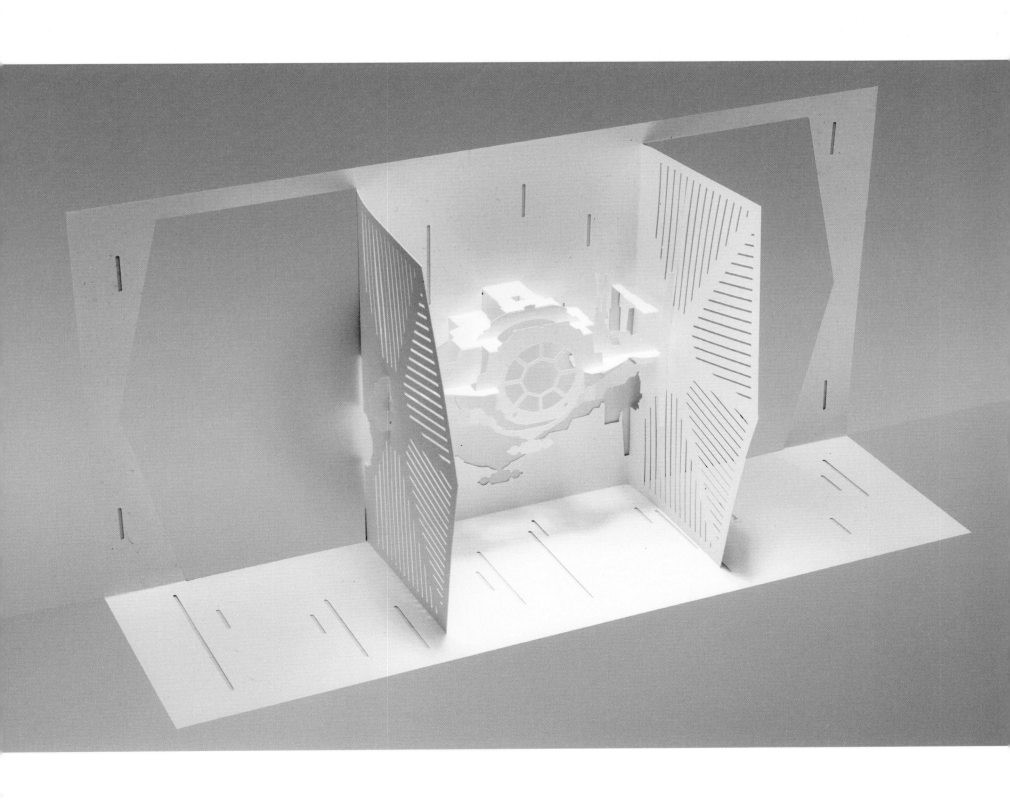

KILO REN'S TIE SILENCER
FROM *STAR WARS* : EPISODE VIII *THE LAST JEDI* (2017)

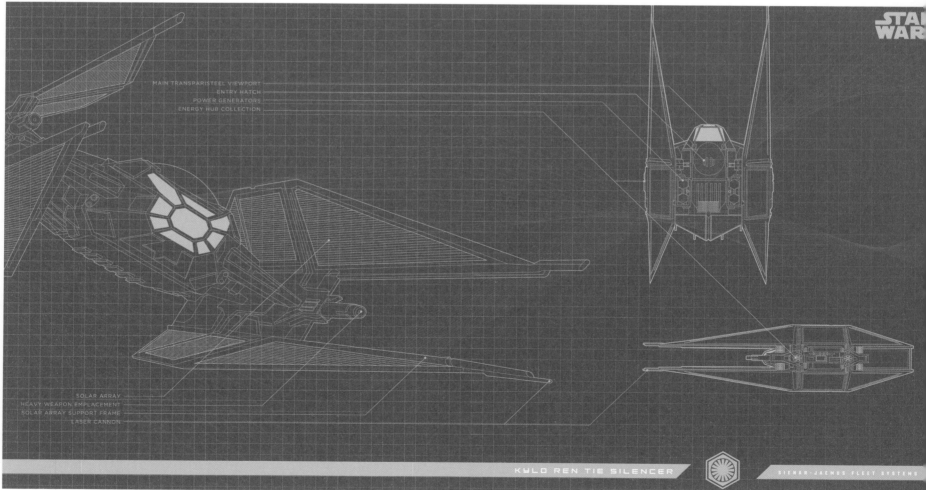

MAIN TRANSPARISTEEL VIEWPORT
ENTRY HATCH
POWER GENERATORS
ENERGY HUB COLLECTION

SOLAR ARRAY
HEAVY WEAPON EMPLACEMENT
SOLAR ARRAY SUPPORT FRAME
LASER CANNON

KYLO REN TIE SILENCER

SIENAR-JAEMUS FLEET SYSTEMS

KILO REN'S TIE SILENCER
FROM *STAR WARS* : EPISODE VIII *THE LAST JEDI* (2017)

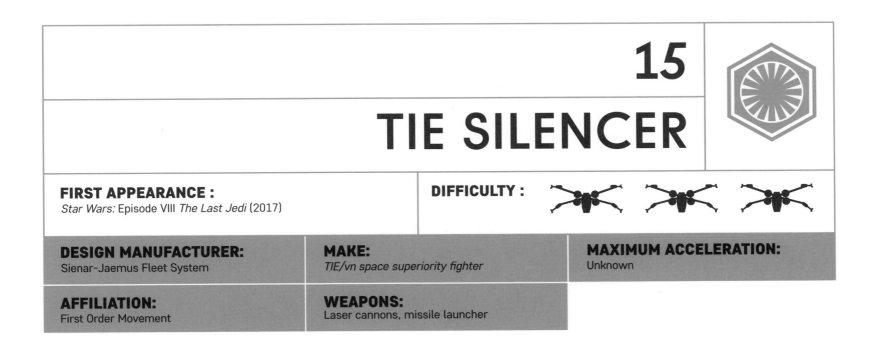

	15	
	TIE SILENCER	

FIRST APPEARANCE :	**DIFFICULTY :**
Star Wars: Episode VIII *The Last Jedi* (2017)	

DESIGN MANUFACTURER:	**MAKE:**	**MAXIMUM ACCELERATION:**
Sienar-Jaemus Fleet System	*TIE/vn space superiority fighter*	Unknown

AFFILIATION:	**WEAPONS:**
First Order Movement	Laser cannons, missile launcher

THERE'S NO SECRET IN KYLO REN'S DESIRE TO EMULATE THE LEGACY OF HIS GRANDFATHER, DARTH VADER.

While Kylo Ren struggles to demonstrate the calculated composure of his ancestor, he exceeds in mimicking his aesthetic. With his dark flowing robes, a foreboding helmet, and an artificial voice, Ren appears in his own personal TIE Advanced x1—known ominously as TIE silencer.

The design of the *Silencer* is an unapologetic homage to Vader's ship. While older models of the TIE fighter are heavily referenced, there are marked differences and enhancements. The infamous spherical cockpit of the older TIE fighter generation, including Vader's, has been replaced with a more angular and elongated nose covered in red glass. The cockpit is reminiscent of Kylo Ren's command shuttle and both of them sharing

similar designs confirms they belong to the dark warrior. The unmistakeable octagonal cockpit window also bears a heavy resemblance to its predecessor, albeit a much more elongated incarnation.

Much like the TIE Advanced x1—Kylo Ren's ship is built around a familiar slab-like body that tapers into a point at the rear end drive units. The most notable feature in Ren's updated ship is the absence of the large octagonal solar panel wings. Its long and pointed replacements are infinitely more hostile. Clearly an evolution of the TIE interceptor, the effect of two long double-prong wings gives Kylo Ren's star fighter a distinctively aggressive guise.

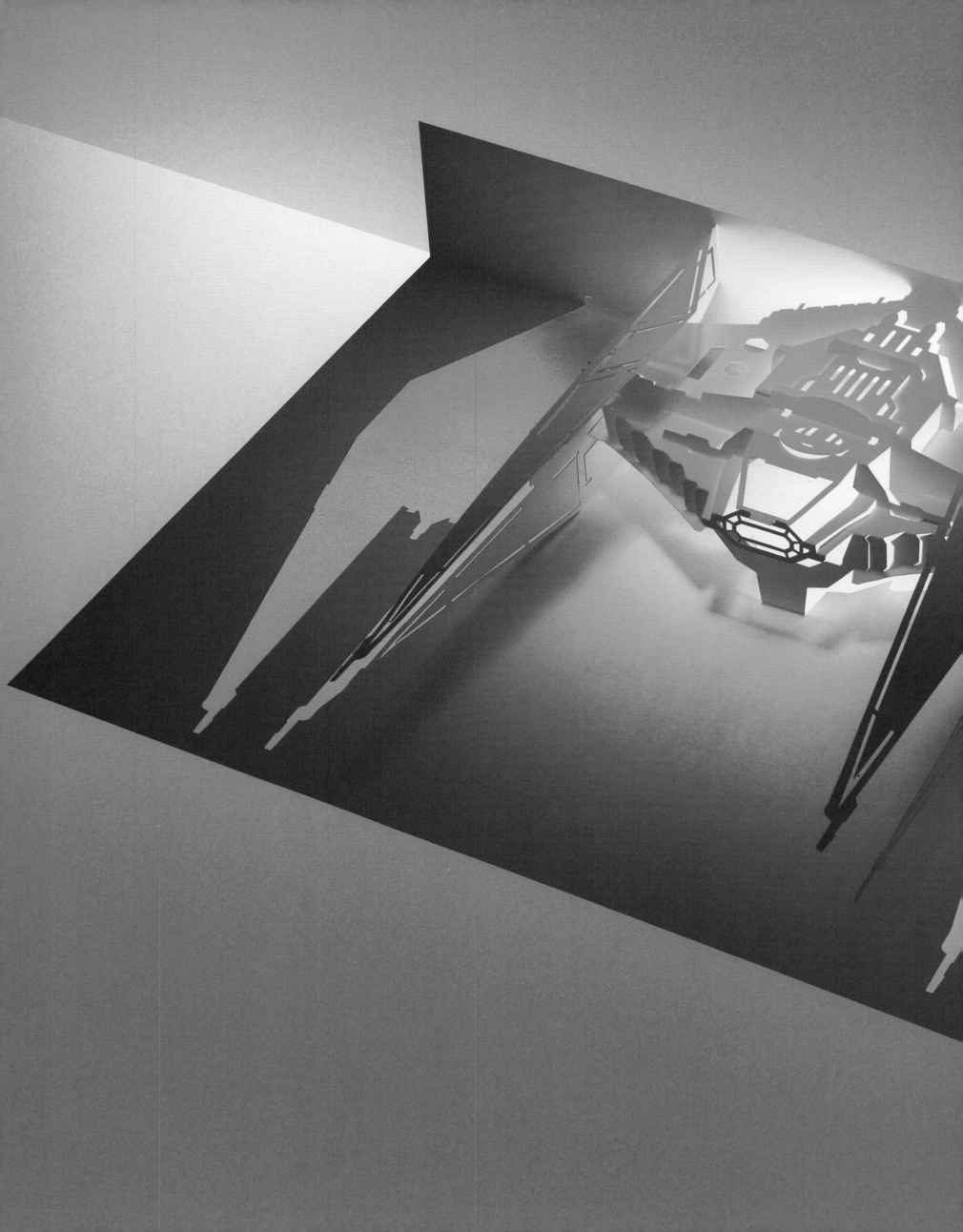

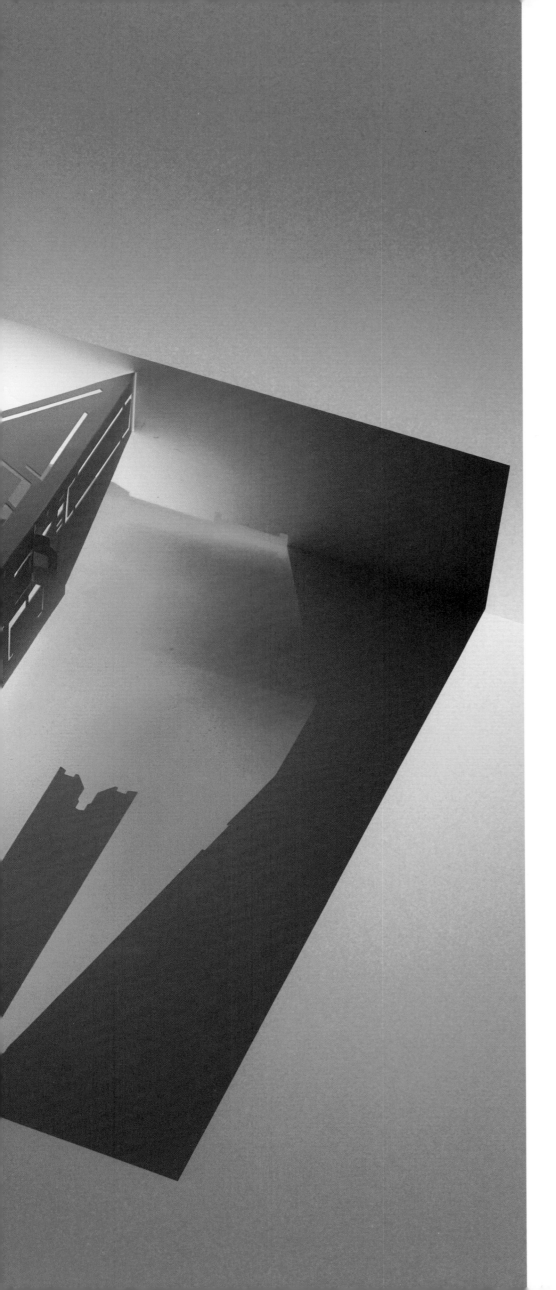

15
—
TIE SILENCER

CUTTING TIPS

Cut and score the template as per the guide section at the beginning of the book. Start with the details on the edges of the wings, followed by the cockpit canopy window. Lots of the folding of this ship will be intuitive. You will tackle clusters of mountain and valley folds at the same time.

FOLDING TIPS

With the paper flat on the table, crease the outer *valley fold* of the wing inward. Unfold and then fold inward the *valley fold* that connects the wing to the *base plate* and then unfold. Do this for both wings.

Take the top portion of the ship's hull in one hand and the mid-portion with the other and push toward each other.

Squeeze the front portion of the wings together.

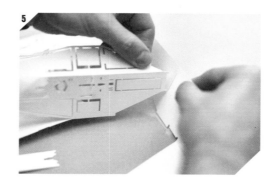

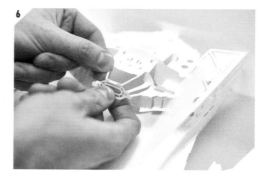

Fold the wings into the upright position again and push through the ends of the wing struts. Fold the small tabs, to keep them secure.

Guide the tabs at the back of the wings through the small slots on the *background plate*. This will help them stay in positon.

Use the small tab at the end of the cockpit canopy to keep it in place.

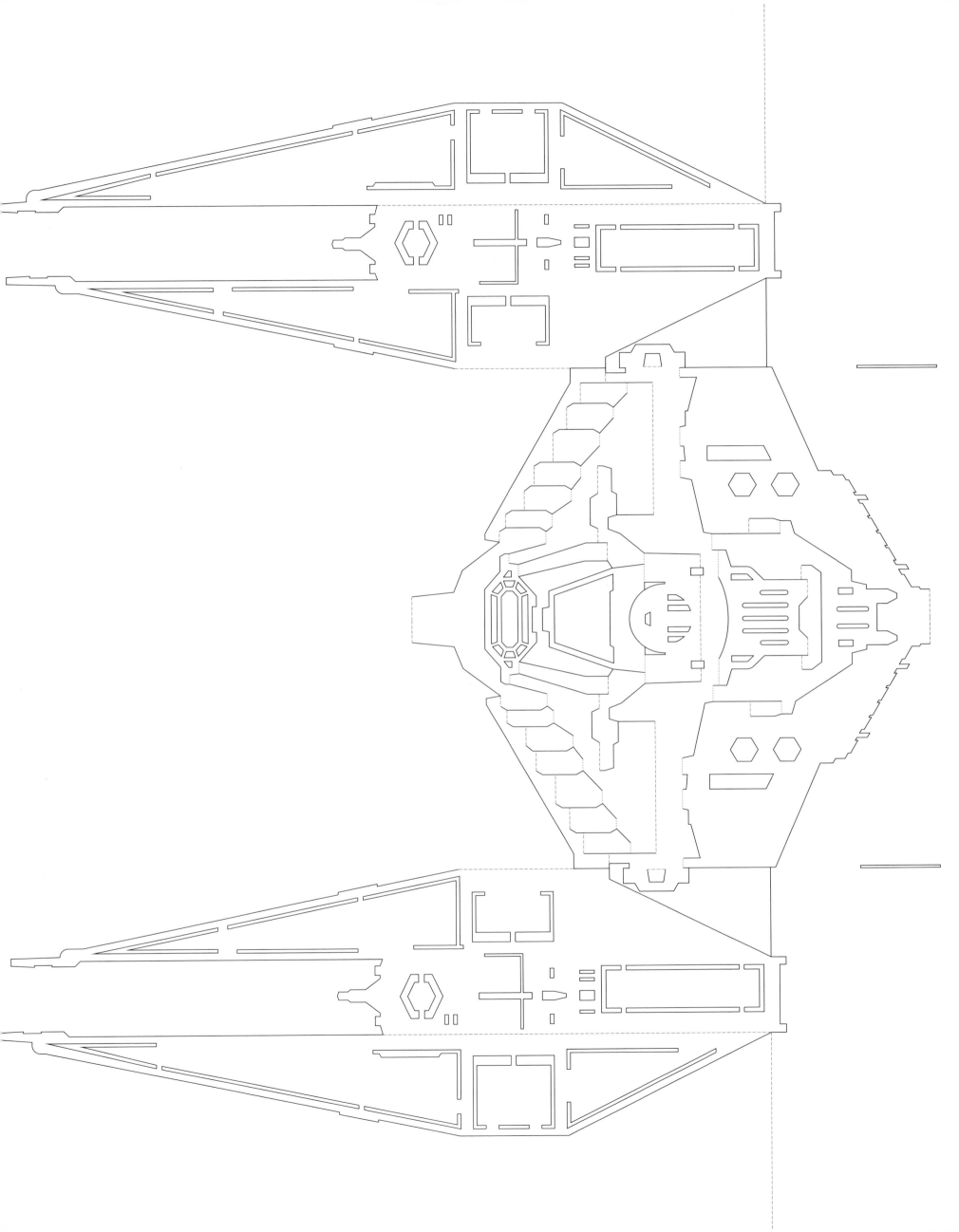

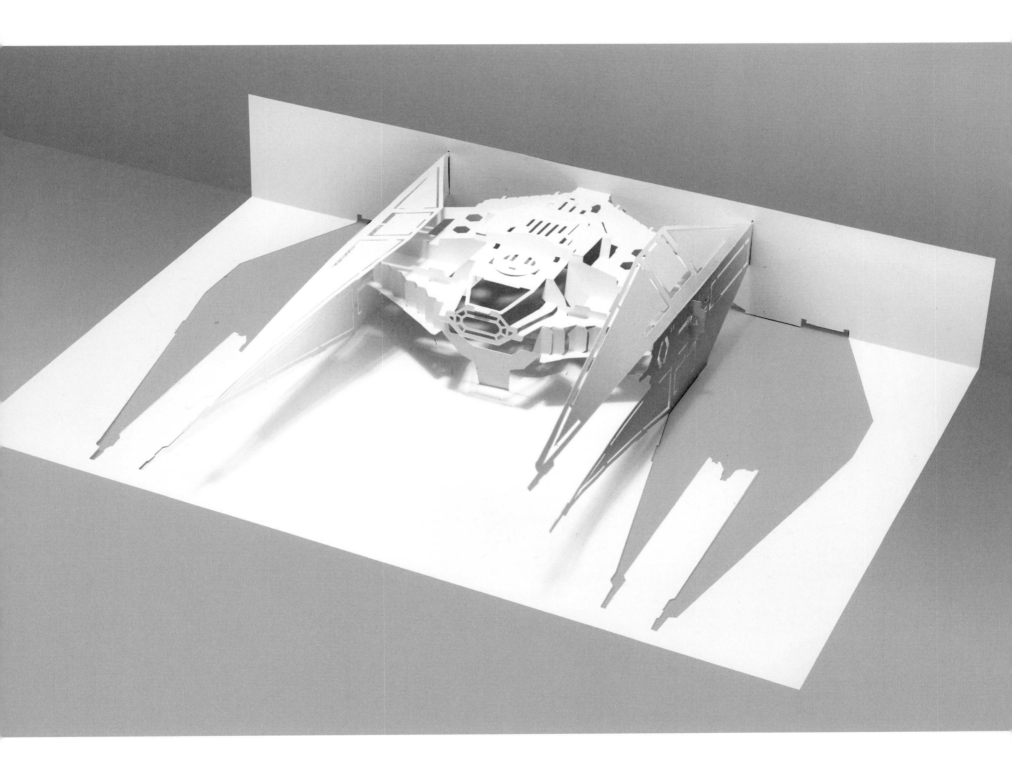

ACKNOWLEDGMENTS

For Jacob Hagan (who thought Jawas were saying "on a peanut" rather than "utinni").

Thank you so much to everyone at Disney, Lucasfilm and Hachette for the constant enthusiasm and encouragement, especially; Michael, Katie, Phil, Jean-Baptiste, Antoine, and everyone else working behind the scenes. Thank you, Shaun for giving me space to spend isolated evenings tinkering with paper. Finally, thanks, J.J., for introducing me to Kathleen!

Marc.

Hachette Heroes would like to thank: Michael Siglain and Frank Parisi from Lucasfilm Publishing, and Olivia Ciancarelli, and Sophie Renard from Disney.

First French edition published in France in 2017 by Hachette Heroes.

First English edition published in the United States in 2017 by Chronicle Books LLC.

Models © 2017 Hachette Heroes, a division of éditions Hachette Pratique. © & TM 2017 Lucasfilm LTD.

ISBN 978-1-4521-6761-9

Manufactured in China
Direction: Catherine Saunier-Talec
Editorial Direction: Antoine Béon
Editor: Jean-Baptiste Roux
Graphic design: Nicole Dassonville
Layout: SKGD-Création

10 9 8 7 6 5 4 3 2 1

See the full range of *Star Wars* book and gift products at www.chroniclebooks.com

Chronicle Books LLC
680 Second Street
San Francisco, CA 94107
www.chroniclebooks.com

www.starwars.com

© & TM 2018 LUCASFILM